A teacher

classroom research

THIRD EDITION

A teacher's guide to classroom research

THIRD EDITION

David Hopkins

Open University Press
Buckingham · Philadelphia

Open University Press
Celtic Court
22 Ballmoor
Buckingham
MK18 1XW

email: enquiries@openup.co.uk
world wide web: www.openup.co.uk

and

325 Chestnut Street
Philadelphia, PA 19106, USA

First edition published 1985, reprinted 1987, 1988, 1990, 1992

Second edition published 1993, reprinted 1994, 1995, 1996, 1998

First published in this third edition 2002

A catalogue record of this book is available from the British Library

ISBN   0 335 21004 X (pb)

Library of Congress Cataloging-in-Publication Data
Hopkins, David, 1949-
    A teacher's guide to classroom research / David Hopkins. – 3rd ed.
        p. cm.
    Includes bibliographical references (p.) and index.
    ISBN 0-335-21004-X
    1. Action research in education.   2. Classroom management–Research.
    3. Observation (Educational method)   4. Curriculum change. I. Title.

    LB1028.24.H67 2001
    370'.7'2–dc21   2001032916

Typeset by Graphicraft Limited, Hong Kong
Printed in Great Britain by Biddles Limited, Guildford and King's Lynn

For
Jeroen, Jessica and Dylan
with love

In short the outstanding characteristic of the extended professional (teacher) is a capacity for autonomous professional self-development through systematic self-study, through the study of the work of other teachers and through the testing of ideas by classroom research procedures.

Lawrence Stenhouse
An Introduction to Curriculum Research and Development

Learning experiences are composed of content, process and social climate. As teachers we create for and with our children opportunities to explore and build important areas of knowledge, develop powerful tools for learning, and live in humanising social conditions.

Bruce Joyce, Emily Calhoun and David Hopkins
Models of Learning – Tools for Teaching

Appreciating a phenomenon is a fateful decision, for it eventually entails a commitment – to the phenomenon and to those exemplifying it – to render it with fidelity and without violating its integrity. Entering the world of the phenomenon is a radical and drastic method of appreciation.

David Matza
Becoming Deviant

And what is good, Phaedrus,
And what is not good –
Need we ask anyone to tell us these things?

Robert Pirsig
Zen and the Art of Motorcycle Maintenance

Contents

Preface to the third edition

The educational landscape in Britain and most other Western countries has changed dramatically since this book was originally published in 1985. The increase in centralized policy-making, however, far from undermining the role of 'teacher researcher', has in my opinion made such a professional ethic all the more necessary. It is becoming increasingly obvious that 'top-down' change does not 'mandate what matters', and that it is local implementation, the work of teachers, that is most influential in determining the achievements of students. If we are serious about enhancing the quality of education in our schools, teachers need to be more, not less, involved in curriculum development, school improvement and pedagogy.

It seems to me that the major differences between now and the mid-1980s is that teacher researchers have increasingly to take a whole school perspective. They now have to interpret and adapt policy to their own teaching situation, to link their classroom research work to that of other colleagues and whole school priorities, as well as to the process of teaching and learning.

In the second edition of *A Teacher's Guide to Classroom Research*, I tried to take this new perspective into account while retaining the structure and simplicity of the original book. In particular, I emphasized the crucial role of classroom observation in supporting teacher and school development, added a new chapter on linking classroom research to other whole school initiatives, updated the text and took the opportunity to rewrite where I had originally been too bland, confused or just got it wrong.

It is a great privilege to have the opportunity to update a book at regular intervals, for it allows one to keep pace with what has proven to be a rapidly changing educational scene. In the second edition I placed more emphasis on the importance of viewing teacher research within a whole school context. In this third edition I argue that not only should teacher research be a whole school activity, but that it should also focus unrelentingly on the teaching and learning process. It has become increasingly apparent to me that if teaching and learning is not the centre-point of our classroom research efforts then the achievement of the young people in our schools will continue to lag behind the aspirations we have for them. And more importantly we will have failed them during the most crucial learning opportunity of their lives. As we pursue an increasingly ambitious educational reform agenda it is vital that we take the opportunity to create a discourse around teaching and learning in our schools and communities.

In the preface for the second edition, I mentioned that since the initial publication of the book I had become the proud father of Jeroen, Jessica and Dylan. Their mother tells me that my writing and practice has become much more learning and classroom focused since they have become part of our lives. Whatever the truth in that, it is certainly the case that as they have developed their own individual learning histories they have consistently challenged my own ideas on education and forced me to rethink and rewrite. As I have written elsewhere, in a profound way, I am continually trying to adjust my educational thinking to keep pace with their development.

What I wish for Jeroen, Jessica and Dylan, is that they not only meet and if possible surpass existing educational standards, but that they also find learning exciting, compelling and intrinsically worthwhile. I wish them to become competent and social beings who have sound, secure and healthy self-concepts to help them face the challenges that await them in their lives. It is here where the personal and the professional converge. What I want for my children is I believe the same as what most teachers wish for their students. There is a striking quality about fine teachers – they care deeply about the young people in their school. Most teachers came into teaching because they wanted to make a difference. Classroom research by teachers is one way of focusing educational efforts to ensure that this difference is being made.

In preparing the third edition of this book, I have taken the opportunity to generally revise and update the text. I have also added some additional examples and cameos that reflect the increased focus on teaching and learning and in a few places I have rearranged certain sections in order to accommodate other necessary revisions. In addition I have completely rewritten the last three chapters. This is to emphasize the contribution classroom research can make to creating a discourse around teaching and learning, to whole school development, and to the creation of increasingly powerful learning communities in our schools.

The book continues to have a modest aim: it is to provide teachers and students with a practical guide to doing research in their own classrooms and to linking these research efforts to the extension of their teaching and learning repertoires and to whole school developments. Despite the proliferation of texts on action research in recent years, I believe that there is still a place for a practical and straightforward introduction to teacher-based classroom research; particularly one that is committed to teacher and school development. In this way, the book complements the existing literature rather than competes with it.

In rereading the book again I was struck once more by how far the original text was influenced by the work of Lawrence Stenhouse and how relevant his ideas still are for us today. Given the great educational challenges that we continue to face, more people of his stature are needed who have a vision of education and can translate it into a coherent philosophy and a pragmatic course of action. On my office wall there is still the quotation from Stenhouse that is on his memorial plaque in the grounds of the University of East Anglia:

> It is teachers who, in the end, will change the world of the school by understanding it.

I hope that in some small way this book continues to contribute to that aspiration.

David Hopkins
Argentiere Mont-Blanc
30th January 2001

Acknowledgements

I am grateful to the late Mike Bruce, Don Cochrane, Peter Norman, Jean Rudduck and especially Ann Kilcher for the care with which they reviewed the original manuscript; and for conversations that clarified my thinking on this and other matters. Their friendship and professional collaboration has meant a great deal to me. Suzzane de Castell, Gill Harper-Jones, Pat Holborn, my sister Mary Schofield, Louise Pelletier and David Pritchard also provided material and intellectual support at critical and opportune times: my thanks to them too. A number of colleagues and students graciously allowed me to use some of their material as illustrations and examples in the first edition. In this regard, I remain indebted to Stan Auerbach, Judy Byer, Heather Lockhard, Sandra Meister, Marianne Schmidt, Ann Waldo and Harvey Walker. The three anonymous reviewers of the original book proposal made comments that encouraged me to revise and improve that manuscript. I anticipate that at least two of them were satisfied with the outcome.

In preparing the second edition of this book, my colleagues at Cambridge were characteristically generous in taking time to review and help me with the manuscript. I am particularly grateful to Mel Ainscow for his thoughtful and creative comments, and more generally for exploring with me the boundaries of professional partnership. Colin Conner, Dave Ebbutt and Julie Howard also reviewed parts of the manuscript and made helpful comments. I am grateful to the Bedfordshire LEA/University of Cambridge Institute of Education 'Developing Successful Learning Project', Howard Bradley and Rob Bollington, Jere Brophy and Tom Good, Walter Doyle, Rex Gibson, David Hargreaves, Pamela Hughes, David Jeffries, Denis Lawton, James McKernan and The Sanders Draper School for letting me use some of their material in this new edition. John Skelton, my publisher at Open University Press, has been most supportive throughout.

The task of preparing the third edition was greatly eased by the assistance of Julie Temperley and John Beresford. They both made numerous and helpful suggestions for updating the text and through our discussions shared with me their own experience of facilitating teacher research. Once again my colleagues have been more than generous in allowing me to include in this new edition work that we have published elsewhere. In this respect I am grateful to Mel Ainscow, John Beresford, David Fulton Publishers, David H. Hargreaves, Alma Harris, David Jackson, Barbara MacGilchrist, Collette Singleton and Ruth Watts. Thanks also to Shona Mullen of the Open University Press who is one of the best, and most supportively critical, editors with whom I have had the pleasure to work.

In the interval between the second and third editions I have had the privilege of working with networks of schools in Nottinghamshire, Derbyshire, Bedfordshire, South Wales, Leicester and Walsall on our 'Improving the Quality of Education For All' school improvement project. This work has focused more than ever before on strategies for teaching and learning and the facilitation of action enquiry and classroom-based research. As always, I have learned a great deal from the commitment, enthusiasm and sheer professionalism of colleagues involved in those networks. It is here that the energy for the transformation of our school system lies. My thanks and admiration to them.

The argument of the book was developed from ideas originally published in the *CARN Bulletin*, the DES booklet *Planning for School Development*, the *Empowered School, Managing Schools Today, Phi Delta Kappan, School Organization* and *The Times Educational Supplement*. Finally, I must also acknowledge the Deakin University Press, the Ford Teaching Project and Universitetsforlaget AS for allowing me to reproduce copyright material.

As always it was Marloes Hopkins de Groot who provided the shelter conditions under which the work could take place: thanks to her for this and many other things.

CHAPTER 1

A teacher's guide to classroom research

This is a practical guide for teachers who wish to undertake research in their classrooms and schools for the purpose of improving practice. Classroom research, in the sense that I refer to it here, is an act undertaken by teachers, to enhance their own or a colleague's teaching, to test the assumptions of educational theory in practice, or as a means of evaluating and implementing whole school priorities. So when I write of classroom research or of the teacher as researcher, I am not envisioning scores of teachers assuming a research role and carrying out research projects to the exclusion of their teaching. My vision is of teachers who have extended their role to include critical reflection upon their craft with the aim of improving it.

Although lip service is often paid to this idea, we live in an educational system that tends to limit individual initiative by encouraging conformity and control. Teachers and pupils (and society too) deserve better than that. Undertaking research in their own and colleagues' classrooms is one way in which teachers can take increased responsibility for their actions and create a more energetic and dynamic environment in which teaching and learning can occur.

The origins of teacher research as a movement can be traced back to the Schools Council's Humanities Curriculum Project (HCP) (1967–72) with its emphasis on an experimental curriculum and the reconceptualization of curriculum development as curriculum research. HCP, in its attempt to encourage a non-partisan and critically reflective attitude to teaching on the part of teachers, had a radical and controversial influence on teaching in British schools during the 1970s.

Following HCP, the concept of teacher research was nurtured by John Elliott and Clem Adelman in the Ford Teaching Project (1972–75). The project involved 40 primary and secondary school teachers in examining their classroom practice through action research. These teachers developed hypotheses about their teaching which could be shared with other teachers and used to enhance their own teaching.

At about the same time, Lawrence Stenhouse, who directed the Humanities Curriculum Project, further popularized the concept of 'the teacher as researcher' by utilizing it as the major theme in his influential book, *An Introduction to Curriculum Research and Development* (Stenhouse 1975). Encouraged by the considerable impact that Stenhouse had on the theory and practice of curriculum and teaching, and the popularity and publicity enjoyed by the Ford Teaching Project, the teacher research movement mushroomed. As well as burgeoning teacher research groups in the UK, Australia, the USA and Canada, there are pockets of teacher-researchers in Scandinavia, France, Chile and many other countries. Although teacher research was not an entirely new concept in the late 1960s, it is from this period that it became an identifiable movement.

Much, however, has changed in the context of education in most Western countries since the concept of the teacher as researcher became popular. The main difference between the 1970s and the first decade of the 21st century is that classroom research has increasingly to be seen within a whole school context. It is no longer sufficient for teachers to do research in their own classrooms, without relating their enquiries to the work of their colleagues and the aims and direction of the school as a whole. We need to strive consciously for a synthesis between teacher research and school development. That is why this book is not just a primer on classroom research techniques, it also attempts to relate teacher research to whole school development.

All books emerge out of a specific set of individual circumstances that have influenced the author, and this book is no exception. The journey that preceded this book is still continuing, and so the story remains unfinished. But two influences in particular have been crucial in developing the ideas presented here and provide a context in which to consider the book. The first is the work of Lawrence Stenhouse. In the Humanities Curriculum Project and his other work, Stenhouse was primarily concerned with the concept of emancipation. He wrote (1983: 163):

> My theme is an old-fashioned one – emancipation . . . The essence of emancipation as I conceive it is the intellectual, moral and spiritual autonomy which we recognise when we eschew paternalism and the role of authority and hold ourselves obliged to appeal to judgement.

There are three levels at which this concept of emancipation can operate – at the level of the student, the teacher and the school.

At the level of the student, emancipation refers to the ability to stand outside the teacher's authority on forms of knowledge, and to discover and own it for oneself. It was in the Humanities Curriculum Project that Stenhouse most notoriously signalled his commitment to this theme. In that project he was principally concerned with the emancipation of pupils through a particular teaching strategy. There were three elements to this aspect of the project: the use of discussion, the use of documents as evidence to inform discussion, and the assumption by the teacher of the role of neutral chairperson. By adopting this approach, Stenhouse was moving away from a teacher-dominated classroom to a setting where pupils, unconstrained by the authority of the teacher, could create meaning for themselves on the basis of evidence and discussion.

If HCP was in part a curriculum designed to emancipate pupils, the phrase 'teacher as researcher' was intended to do the same for teachers. Teachers are too often the servants of heads, advisers, researchers, textbooks, curriculum developers, examination boards or the Department for Education and Skills, among others. By adopting a research stance, teachers are liberating themselves from the control and command situation they often find themselves in. Stenhouse encouraged teachers to follow the specification of a curriculum or teaching strategy, but at the same time to assess it critically. Such curriculum proposals and teaching specifications are probably intelligent but are not necessarily correct. Their effectiveness should therefore be monitored by teachers in the classroom. By adopting this critical approach, by taking a research stance, the teacher is engaged not only in a meaningful professional development activity, but also engaged in a process of refining, and becoming more autonomous in, professional judgement. This applies as much to the National Curriculum as it did to the HCP.

The third level at which emancipation can operate is that of the school. Here it is a question of the school liberating itself from a bureaucratic educational system. The image of the 'ideal' type of emancipated school is represented by the words 'autonomous', 'creative', 'moving' or 'problem-solving'. These successful schools take the opportunity of the recent changes and use them to support developments already underway or planned for in the school. They adapt external change for internal purposes. In the most successful or emancipated schools, there is also a realization that successful change involves learning on the part of teachers. This implies that successful change strategies involve a seamless web of activities that focus on, are integrated with and enhance the daily work of teachers. This can result in quite profound alterations to the culture of the school and the ways in which teachers, heads and governors work together towards the goal of student achievement.

The second influence on this book is more personal. During the 1970s, I trained as a teacher and taught, worked as an Outward Bound instructor and mountain guide, and read for postgraduate degrees in education. Although somewhat different activities, they were all characterized by a desire, often hesitant and naive, to create ways in which people could take more control of their own lives. Irrespective of the context – practice teaching, an 'O' level history class, counselling a 'delinquent' pupil, assisting in a youth club, on the rock face, out in the wilderness, or discussing ideas in a seminar – there were similarities in overall aim and pedagogic structure.

Later, as a teacher in a Canadian university, I taught courses in curriculum development, analysis of teaching, classroom research, and found in Stenhouse's work a theoretical framework within which I could put my ideas into action. The book emerged from that experience, more specifically from a course I taught in classroom research and some papers I wrote on the topic (Hopkins 1982, 1984a,b). Thus, the book is based on a set of ideas that have the enhancement of teacher judgement and autonomy as a specific goal, and is grounded within the practical realities of teachers and students.

This interest in classroom-based work, although always in my mind linked to school improvement, has assumed a broader perspective whilst at Cambridge and Nottingham. Much of this work has been concerned with assisting teachers, schools and local education authorities (LEAs) to handle and reflect on the change process. I have learned an enormous amount from them, as I did from my involvement in the evaluation of TVEI, the DES projects on Teacher Appraisal and School Development Plans, and in particular our school improvement project 'Improving the Quality of Education for All'. I have also been fortunate to have worked over a slightly longer period with the OECD's Centre for Educational Research and Innovation on a number of school improvement-related projects. This work has helped me to see the teacher's role in the wider context of the school as an organization and workplace. In particular, it has impressed on me the crucial importance of the culture of the school in sustaining teacher development.

It is this commitment to a practical philosophy of emancipation and empowerment as well as a particular set of individual circumstances that underpin the argument in this book. After this introduction, a few case studies of teacher-based research are given to provide a context for what follows. In Chapter 3, two arguments are considered for teacher-based research – the need for professionalism in teaching, and the inadequacy of the traditional research approach in helping teachers improve their classroom practice. In Chapter 4, action research, which has become the main vehicle for teacher research, is discussed and critiqued; from that discussion, six criteria for teacher-based research are suggested. Chapter 5 discusses the ways in which teacher research problems are formulated and initiated. Chapters 6 and 7 describe the principles and practice of classroom observation, and in Chapter 8 various other ways of gathering information on classroom behaviour are described. Chapter 9 outlines a method for analysing these data. These five chapters constitute the heart of the teacher research process. In Chapter 10 there is an elaboration of the explicit focus of the third edition on teaching and learning. In arguing that pedagogy should become the heartland of classroom research, I review the research on effective teaching and models of teaching and provide practical examples of three common models of learning and teaching. The discussion in Chapter 11 highlights the role of development planning as a vehicle for linking classroom research activities to school improvement strategies in the pursuit of enhanced learning outcomes for students. In the final chapter, I stand back a little and attempt briefly to connect the discussion in previous chapters to the themes of teacher and school development, in particular the creation of a culture that promotes networks and professional learning communities within and outside the school.

A continuing emphasis throughout the book is the importance of establishing a professional ethic for teaching. Implicit in this idea is the concept of teacher as researcher. The teacher-researcher image is a powerful one. It embodies a number of characteristics that reflect on the individual teacher's capacity to be in Stenhouse's phrase 'autonomous in professional judgement'. A major factor in this is the teacher's ability to think systematically and critically about what he or she is doing and to collaborate with other teachers. Central to this activity is the systematic reflection on one's classroom experience, to understand it and to create meaning out of that understanding. By becoming self-conscious, collaborative and critical about their teaching, teachers develop more power over their professional lives, extend their teaching repertoires, and are better able to create classrooms and schools that are responsive to the vision they and we have for our children's future.

FURTHER READING

The key source for any teacher-researcher is the work of Lawrence Stenhouse, in particular his *An Introduction to Curriculum Research and Development* (1975). Although he died before making his own comprehensive statement on classroom research by teachers, Jean Rudduck and I (Rudduck and Hopkins 1985) edited his published and unpublished writing to make such an argument in *Research as a Basis for Teaching*. Until the mid-1980s most of the work on teacher research was either philosophical discussion (Kemmis 1983, 1988), reports by researchers (Elliot and Adelman 1976) or teachers' own accounts of their research (Nixon 1981). Since that time, however, there has been a dramatic growth in the number of books on the topic. Pride of place must go to John Elliott's (1991) *Action Research for Educational Change*, which traces the development of the teacher research movement, describes its methodology and explores how it can be 'a form of creative resistance' to centralized policy-making. Other books that attempt in different ways to link the ethic of teacher research to school development and educational change are Helen Simons' (1987) *Getting to*

Know Schools in Democracy, Rob Halsall's (1998) collections on *Teacher Research and School Improvement*, our own *The Empowered School* (Hargreaves and Hopkins 1991) and *The New Structure of School Improvement* (Joyce *et al.* 1999). Much else of relevance to the theme of 'classroom research by teachers' has been published recently, and I have referred to them in the 'Further Reading' section at the end of the most appropriate chapter.

CHAPTER 2

Classroom research in action

Often the phrase classroom research brings to mind images of white-coated (or grey-suited!) educational researchers undertaking research in a sample of schools or classrooms and using as subjects the teachers and students who live out their educational lives within them. Often this image is correct. This book, however, is about another kind of research in which teachers look critically at their own classrooms primarily for the purpose of improving their teaching and the quality of education in their schools. But even the phrase 'classroom research by teachers' can sound a little daunting. It might be useful therefore to begin with some examples of teachers who have engaged in systematic self-conscious enquiry with the purpose of understanding and improving their practice.

The first four cases were all written by the teachers who were themselves involved in the classroom research. The first two were prepared by teachers with whom I worked in British Columbia. They contrast well with each other: the first is an exploratory case study undertaken by a beginning teacher; the second is more focused, and reflects the confidence of a teacher experienced in classroom research. The second pair of examples were written by teachers involved in the University of Cambridge Institute of Education and Bedfordshire Education Service 'Developing Successful Learning' Project. Besides describing different methodologies, they also illustrate the benefits of using partnerships in classroom research.

The third pair of examples reflect the focus in this third edition of the book on teaching and learning and school improvement. The first by John Beresford, the research officer on the IQEA project, describes how he collaborates with schools in providing data on teaching and learning styles to assist in defining the focus of their improvement strategies. The second is by David Jackson who, at the time of writing the cameo, was Head of a longstanding IQEA School, Sharnbrook Upper School and Community

College in Bedfordshire. (David is now Head of Research at the National College for School Leadership.) This vignette describes how the school improvement focus on teaching and learning is organized at Sharnbrook, and how students are involved in the process.

The final example is different from the others in a number of ways; in particular, it illustrates the use of 'quantitative' as opposed to the more usual 'qualitative' methods in teacher-based classroom research. It was also written by Lawrence Stenhouse.

In each of these cases, the teachers are engaging in classroom research for the express purpose of improving the quality of educational life in their classroom. This is no deficit model of improvement, however; the teachers involved are genuinely interested in understanding the dynamics of their own teaching style. They believe that you do not have to be ill to get better. The motivation for doing so may be varied – a research degree, natural curiosity, a stimulating article or talk – but the process and its implications are essentially the same. Taken together, these cases illustrate the range and benefits of doing research in your own classroom and provide examples of the reflective professional in practice.

The first example is a case study by Sandra Meister, when she was a first year teacher in Prince George, British Columbia.

The purpose of this research project is to become familiar with educational research within the classroom, to analyse and improve one aspect of my teaching style. But I have had some difficulty in pinpointing which aspect of my teaching I wished to focus on. As a harried first year teacher, I really had not given much time to actually thinking about the way I taught; rather, I tended to worry about keeping things peaceful until the three o'clock bell rang. I decided, however, to look at the types of questions I asked, the order in which I asked them, and to whom the questions were directed. This sequence appears to be the key to training a child to think independently. In order to become more aware of my own teaching style, I decided to obtain data from myself as teacher, from my class and from an outside observer who was previously unknown to myself and my students.

Social studies was an area I find particularly dull at this level. The entire primary curriculum centres around 'myself and my family in our community', 'components of our community' and, finally, 'the interaction of communities'. The lessons I had taught were rather scattered and poorly sequenced. As a final unit, I decided to divide the class into three groups and have one group research communities of the past, one look at Prince George as it is today and one group design a community for the future. Most of the knowledge came from group lessons and discussions where, through various questions and brainstorming techniques, I hoped to direct the student to some logical conclusions as to the necessary requirements for community life.

The lesson used as the basis for the research was on different modes of communication. I taught the lesson while the observer recorded the types of questions asked (i.e. fact, critical thinking, explanation, yes/no, etc.), which students responded and the teacher reaction to the response. The data were gathered by the observer using a checklist. The lesson was also audio-taped, which enabled both the teacher and the observer to review the data afterwards.

The results were really quite an eye opener. The majority of my questions required critical thinking or an opinion, whereas the remainder were questions for the purpose of gathering facts. Most of the questions required one- or two-word answers. The following is an analysis of my questioning techniques.

Types of questions asked: on the positive side, most of the questions required critical thinking, i.e. 'How would you feel . . . ?', 'What would you do if . . . ?' Many questions required students to express an opinion; I avoided Yes/No questions, which is something I was pleased to note. On the negative side, I seemed to avoid asking any questions which required any type of explanation. This is an important area which I have overlooked.

Sequence of questions asked: the order in which the questions were asked seemed logical and new information was built on previous answers. The weakest area here seemed to be in moving from one topic to the next. I'll need to work on having a few key questions as pivot points for my lesson.

To whom questions were directed: on the positive side, I would often ask one question, such as 'Who do you talk to on the phone?', and randomly choose many students for a one-word answer which keeps them all involved and interested. On the negative side, whenever I asked an open question, I seemed to respond to one of three students regardless of who may have had their hands up. These particular students are those with whom I try to avoid confrontations.

Teacher responses to answers: this is the area which I feel this project has identified as something for me to question. As I looked at the data, I realized that I rarely praised the students verbally. The majority of teacher responses were repeating what the child said and nodding to affirm their stance. The next frequent teacher response was no reaction. The students, however, seemed satisfied with the way their opinions were accepted without much comment and didn't appear to act differently when verbal praise was given. I also appeared to accept an answer regardless of whether hands were up or not.

There are three areas where there are possibilities for improvement. The first is to accept answers and request answers from all students rather than a select few. An obvious way to improve this is to limit the size of the group to whom the lesson is being taught. Perhaps using a phrase such as 'let's let someone else have a turn' would help. The changes need not be large and I'm glad this was brought to my attention – imagine some poor child spending a year in my class and never being asked a question!

The second area for change is in making a smooth transition from one topic to the next within a lesson. I feel this can be accomplished by noting beforehand a comparison phrase or question and recording differences or similarities between the two topics.

Finally, I must learn to allow the children an opportunity to give detailed explanations. This is an ideal opportunity for improving verbal lucidity and compositional skills.

The next time I conduct or participate in a research project, I will use the 'triangulation approach'. The insight of an outside observer will be invaluable and will allow the students to offer some feedback. I would also like to participate in a project where the observer would be the director (adviser) and have more than one classroom involved. By playing a small role in a larger-scale project, I feel I would gain more first-hand knowledge and become confident in being a teacher researcher.

The second case study is by Ann Waldo, an experienced teacher who had previously been involved in classroom research.

Bruce Joyce and Beverly Showers (1984) maintain that when given adequate training conditions, teachers are consistently able to fine-tune existing skills and learn new ones. However, they point out that learning a new skill does not guarantee being able to transfer a skill vertically to higher-order, more complex tasks. Early-task learning has been found to maximize transfer if the tasks are relevant to the acquisition of a teaching model.

My school district has been encouraging teachers to use cognitive models of teaching. Bloom's Taxonomy and the Renzuli Triad Model have specifically been suggested as the models to be used to provide an enriched curriculum. Last year, teachers had in-service training on these approaches and this included theory and demonstration with adults. The demonstration teams were young, enthusiastic and well-prepared fellow teachers. The teachers went back to their classrooms ready to implement higher-order thinking. Despite using devices such as specific question words to elicit different levels of responses, most teachers found it very difficult to do this.

After watching a videotape of myself teaching and failing to allow students think-time before responding, I wondered if this inability in an early task could have caused some of the difficulties I experienced in using Bloom's Taxonomy and Renzuli's Triad Model, as both models are dependent on students' ability to articulate their thoughts. Verbalizing high-level thinking demands that time is spent formulating the response. The other two primary teachers in my school had only moderate success in implementing the new models.

I decided that for this piece of research I would ask these teachers consciously to extend think-time to the recommended 3–5 seconds. I hypothesized that this would lead to lengthier student responses and higher-order questions from the teacher. Hopefully, the teachers would also begin to internalize this early-task learning and be better equipped to implement other models of teaching that are dependent on student response.

The subjects were a grade 1 teacher (S1) who has taught for 27 years and a grade 2 teacher (S2) who has taught for 14 years. Both agreed to audiotape a session of directed reading to provide baseline data. They were informed that they would be asked to alter one aspect of their teaching which, in turn, was expected to cause a change to occur. It was decided that allowing the teachers to audiotape themselves would disturb students and teachers less than an observer or a videotape. S2 taped a group with low academic ability; S1 taped a group with average ability.

The baseline tapes were interpreted by myself. Think-time between each teacher question and response was recorded. If a response came less than 1 second after the question, it was designated 0 seconds. The number of words in each student response was counted. Each question was related to level 1, 2, 3, 4, 5 or 6 responses according to Bloom's Taxonomy. The hierarchy in Bloom's Taxonomy is: 1, knowledge; 2, comprehension; 3, application; 4, analysis; 5, synthesis; 6, evaluation. As S1 had taped only 13 questions and responses, I decided to use the first 10 questions on each tape, provided they were not repetitions or rephrasings.

These data were discussed with the teachers on the following day except for the hierarchical rating of the questions. This was not mentioned. They were asked to read an excerpt from 'Extending think-time for better reading instruction' by Linda Gambrell (1981). In this excerpt, the author stresses that the teacher must be prepared for leaden silences and resist the temptation to fill them. The student must also be prepared by the teacher to accept the think-time for thinking instead of unproductive hand-waving in the belief that responding is a speed competition. Lastly, she stresses that it takes time for teachers and students to slow down. There was no mention of higher levels of questions or responses.

The teachers, therefore, were set to extend think-time in the hope of lengthening student responses. They were asked to tape themselves three more times with the same reading groups, but it was explained that these tapes would be used for self-monitoring rather than as data. They were encouraged to extend think-time whenever appropriate in the classroom in order to get more practice.

Six school days after the baseline data had been collected, the teachers were again asked to tape their guided reading in order to provide data for the research. They were reminded to use the same reading groups as for the baseline data. The data from these tapes were used in exactly the same manner as the baseline tapes.

For both teachers, there was an increase in the length of student response when think-time was increased (see Table 2.1). There was also a small increase in the hierarchical level of questions posed to the students by the teachers. These results cannot be said to be statistically significant because of the size of sample, but they do replicate other findings. The results would seem to indicate that teachers automatically ask more stimulating questions when they are consciously trying to increase student input into discussions.

One of the problems in the research design was that it did not allow for differences in conceptual ability. A teacher automatically adjusts level of questions according to the ability of the group. S2 could not change her level of questions too much because of the conceptual level of the group. S1 had an average group and could, therefore, hope to have higher-level responses even though the children were younger.

Table 2.1   Relationship between model of teaching and learning skills

	Teacher	Think-time[a] (seconds)	Responses[a] (words)	Level[a]
Baseline	S1	0.1	2.4	1.2
	S2	1.0	3.5	1.4
Post-test	S1	2.5	4.6	1.5
	S2	3.2	6.3	1.5

[a] Average over ten questions.

If I had had more time, I would have analysed far more data for each teacher and increased the number of teachers and done another piece of research to discover if there was any transfer effect using an information-processing model of teaching.

The third case describes how three teachers used a process of mutual support and observation to change teaching and learning experiences in their classrooms. Two of them, Sheelagh Sullivan and Liz Satherly, were teachers working in Samuel Whitbread Upper School. The third member of the group, Jackie Markham, had worked with teachers in the school as part of her role with the Special Education Support Service.

The partnership between Liz and Sheelagh developed because Sheelagh, as a learning support teacher, had worked in the classroom with Liz, a teacher of Humanities. Liz was a relatively new entrant to the profession and keen to develop more successful learning in her classroom. Sheelagh and Jackie were both keen to look at support for learning as a way of meeting individual needs.

Sheelagh and Liz had an informal meeting to discuss those aspects of their practice that they hoped to explore. Liz wanted to look at her classroom management and Sheelagh was concerned with effective group work. We also organized suitable times, lessons and classes for observation. It was difficult to fit in all of the desired observations, so Jackie offered to assist by taking on three of the observations. We spent some time discussing suitable observation techniques and decided that, to look at group work, we needed to use a video.

We wanted the opportunity to include some feedback from the students and so a last minute decision was made to use a brief questionnaire. A published questionnaire was used, but on reflection it would have been better to have constructed our own.

The observations took place over a period of two weeks. Four of Liz's lessons were observed, two by Sheelagh and two by Jackie. Three of Sheelagh's were observed, one by Jackie and two by Liz using a video for the final observation. The observations went well, the only difficulty being the lack of time for immediate feedback at the end of the lesson. The subsequent review meeting took longer than we had expected. It should have been obvious that a video of a one-hour lesson would take the same amount of time to watch!

In both cases, a descriptive feedback of the lesson was given. We avoided judgemental comments, although this sometimes felt impersonal. Both classroom teachers felt the need to hear about successful aspects of the lesson. They were able to identify specific areas of their practice where change could lead to more successful student learning.

Three roles developed during the course of these meetings: teacher, observer and 'critical friend'. These roles were interchangeable, but the critical friend tended to be the person who was able to ask leading questions that enabled the teacher to clarify her thinking and make decisions about the action she would take. Liz decided that she would give written instructions at the start of the lesson but would also provide supportive oral reinforcement at planned intervals. Sheelagh decided to remove barriers to communication by reorganizing seating arrangements and reducing group size. At this stage, it would have been useful to look at the questionnaires, but there had not been enough time to tabulate the results.

Liz and Sheelagh agreed to one further observation of each other's lessons, which would be followed by a meeting to reflect upon what had been achieved. Sheelagh managed to observe the lesson as planned, but practical obstacles made it impossible for Liz to reciprocate. However, we met as intended. It proved a very positive meeting. Sheelagh gave feedback to Liz and provided a self-evaluation of her own lesson. Many of the comments made at this stage were judgemental, but because of the level of trust and confidence that had been established, we didn't find this threatening. Also, because the discussion was so open, Jackie's role as critical friend disappeared.

Generally, we felt pleased with what had been achieved. Liz was convinced that the quality of coursework assignments produced by the group observed had improved. Further observations would be difficult to arrange, but it was felt that partnerships had been established through which an open discussion of teaching and learning experiences in our classrooms would be possible.

The fourth case was prepared by Pamela Hughes, a teacher of English and Sharnbrook Upper School's Individual Needs Co-ordinator.

During our initial 'chats', we decided that we would like to involve our students as much as possible; we were all learners. We were nervous about how the students would react to this approach, especially one class which contained some very 'strong characters', but we felt that it was important for us to involve them.

During the lesson prior to the observation, the students were asked to make lists of all the things that (a) helped and (b) hindered their understanding and learning in school, not just the class they were in for that lesson. There was a short class brainstorm before dividing into groups of four. The students, without exception, were animated and very enthusiastic and did not use this as an opportunity to be vindictive. The results gave us a useful insight into the students' perceptions of their learning as well as forming a 'learning bond' between us.

The observation

My lesson to be observed was a Year 9 English class of 30 students, who would be working in groups carrying out tasks associated with beginnings of stories. I arrived to find no class, a sixth-former who had come to support without my prior knowledge, the furniture completely rearranged, a lack of chairs and my partner ready to observe my lesson! Once these minor setbacks had been overcome, I was ready to begin. I felt very conscious of another person in the very small claustrophobic room and I found myself being very careful about what I said and how I said it, but within a few minutes I had forgotten that I was being observed.

Christine wrote down a 'description' of my lesson, using words and diagrams, a mirror image, that we would use together for the Review. Immediately after the lesson, Christine thanked me for letting her observe my lesson and I felt relaxed and reassured. We confirmed our time for the Review.

The review

We decided to meet after school in Christine's classroom where we knew that we would not be disturbed. We reflected on my lesson and I did not feel threatened by the discussion. I began by giving my view of the lesson and then gradually we drew out areas that I could develop. I had challenged the able pupils by questioning, but the weaker students may have benefited from key ideas and words being put on the board to enable them to contribute more easily to their group discussions. Christine had noticed that one pair seemed 'inadequate' until the second task when they joined with another pair, and even then the four were not as creative or perceptive as the other groups. She also noticed an individual student on the fringes of his group discussion.

The action phase

I decided to review and develop two aspects of my teaching: my use of the board as a learning resource (not only within group work) and the management of groups within the class. My aim was to enable all students to participate fully when doing cooperative group tasks. To help evaluate whether these areas of development would be effective, we decided that I would give a questionnaire to the students as soon as possible and again during the second half of the term. I would monitor the progress of the three students mentioned by Christine. Also, a further observation would take place.

The reflection

Since our initial observations, Christine and I often discuss aspects of our lessons, not only those of our Action Plan, sharing success as well as conferring when needing support. We are at the stage of evaluating our initial Action Plans and feel confident that we will continue our partnership as we feel that we have learnt from each other and the students.

Christine's thoughts

I had worked in an Australian system where peer assessment was used in conjunction with appraisal by the senior management, in order to be re-licensed or promoted. This also involved a great deal of paperwork at first; therefore, I was apprehensive about forming a partnership with Pamela.

In fact, it has been like an 'ego-massage'! As teachers, we seldom have the opportunity of hearing another teacher's view of our classroom, or of observing another class ourselves. It has been a wonderful opportunity to recall success and discuss 'failures'. It has made us find time to listen and support each other; unless you make time there isn't any.

Our department is very open and people other than teachers and class members are often in the classroom, but this was different – it was for us. We were able to look at our teaching and the students in a different light. I was aware of a temptation to 'play to the new adult audience', but this disappeared quickly. The most singular thing to me is how memorable that lesson was; I feel that heightening my awareness at the time has helped memory of it to remain vivid.

When I went into Pamela's lesson I was a little apprehensive. I knew that I could walk into any of her lessons, but this was different as I felt that I was watching for something – looking for some area to define and not being certain what it was. This proved to be an unfounded concern. I mirrored the lesson as I saw it and we had plenty to review and debate.

We learnt from each other, opening up many possibilities. The lessons I observed and those I was observed in, are imprinted on my mind.

In this vignette, John Beresford, the research officer on the IQEA project, describes how he collaborates with schools in providing data on styles teaching and learning to assist in defining the focus of their improvement strategies.

There is already an extensive literature on the component parts of effective teaching (see, for example, Chapter 10) but less on the process of matching teaching strategies to students' learning styles. Much of the matching of teaching and learning styles has been extremely speculative, based upon the premise that if a sufficient variety of strategies are employed, then a catch-all effect will apply.

The need for some form of dialogue between teachers and students about teaching and learning methods in the classroom has increasingly been recognized by a number of the schools in the IQEA project. These schools have shown themselves willing to discuss with students their views about what constitutes effective teaching. It is also clear that they regard some acknowledgement of student learning preferences, in the teaching which takes place within their classrooms, as an element of effective teaching in its own right. They have also called for an easy-to-administer research instrument that can both help them match what goes on in classrooms more closely to the preferences of their students and provide clues about where to develop the teaching repertoire of their teachers and the learning repertoire of their students.

In order to undertake an audit of the teaching strategies used in its classrooms, and a survey of students' views on those strategies, we developed instruments based on the work of David Kolb. Kolb's (1984) seminal work, *Experiential Learning*, effectively reconceptualizes Piaget's work on developmental learning into four distinct and authentic learning styles, with no implicit hierarchical structure. These four learning styles can be represented as quadrants in a grid where the two dimensions of perceiving and processing information have been juxtaposed, and Kolb also gives useful descriptors of each learning style.

Our colleagues have further identified a range of classroom activities and strategies associated with each of the four learning styles (see Fielding 1994) and from this have produced an observation schedule which can be used to record the incidence of these various activities in a lesson (Beresford 1998). Each activity is coded according to the learning style for which it caters. As each activity occurs in the lesson, its incidence is noted. No assessment is attempted regarding the effectiveness of the various strategies within the context of the lesson. At the end of the period of observation the different number of strategies and learning activities employed by the teacher is totted up and recorded, in the boxes provided, against the appropriate learning style. Hence the lesson can be said to have a particular profile corresponding to the combination of numbers in the boxes. These can be converted into percentages of the total number of strategies and activities used.

In order to assess students' preferences for these characteristics teaching activities, we drew up a similar schedule on which students were asked to indicate which of the activities they preferred. The schedule consists of a list of classroom activities directly related to the teaching strategies listed in the observation schedule. By scoring 'Don't Like' responses as 0, 'Don't Mind' as 1 and 'Like' as 2 and adding the total for each of the learning style categories, a profile similar to that derived from lesson observations can be derived for each student. By adding the totals of all students in a particular group, a group profile can be obtained. These profiles indicate individual and group learning style preferences (see Beresford 1998, 1999).

The schedule is versatile inasmuch as it can be used to gauge individual's learning preferences as well as group ones. Students' preferences in individual subjects can be assessed as well as their general learning preferences. Some schools have used the schedules to find out which strategies the students feel are most effective in the teaching of an individual subject, but most have felt that their students lack the necessary analytical skills to arrive at such a judgement. The schedule can also be used to assess any gender differences or differences between year groups.

In this example, David Jackson who, at the time of writing the cameo, was Head of Sharnbrook Upper School and Community College in Bedfordshire, describes how the school improvement focus on teaching and learning is organized at Sharnbrook, and how students are involved in the process.

Sharnbrook Upper School and Community College was established as a 13–19 upper school in 1975 to provide comprehensive education for 32 villages situated in rural mid-England. Sharnbrook's school improvement model is now a continuous, whole-school initiative deeply embedded into our work. At its heart is a fluid group (cadre) of staff committed to working in partnerships and together around areas of mutually agreed enquiry. During the eight years of involvement with IQEA we have had almost as many different modes of operation for the school improvement group, but certain characteristics remain consistent. Some of these are that:

- The school improvement group is led by two staff operating in a co-leadership model.
- The school improvement group breaks down into trios of staff, each engaged in a separate enquiry designed to generate knowledge and understanding about the school's work and to indicate directions for improvement.
- Each of these partnerships undertakes a sustained process of enquiry within the school, drawing also from the knowledge-base within the field and from good practice elsewhere, and, as an outcome of this data-gathering, suggests improvement to the school's practice, supports the implementation of improvements and then enquires further into their effect upon student learning or the wider school community.
- Each partnership tries to ensure that all those who contribute towards their research are involved, too, in the process of making meaning from the data and, where feasible, in the implementation of outcomes.
- Each partnership also commits to connect with the wider constituency of staff, students, parents and governors in order that all who need to do so can share the emergent journey.
- The school facilitates opportunities for each partnership to lock into consultation and decision-making structures, as appropriate, so that findings from the enquiry will be implemented.
- The entire school improvement group commits to monitoring the value of their own work and to critique each other's practice.

It goes without saying that staff at all levels of the school are involved, including newly qualified teachers, support staff and, more recently, students. Each partnership is entirely free of status positions within the more formal organizational structure of the school and offers leadership opportunities to a variety of staff. Some partnerships might be involved with significant whole-school issues (for example, assessment strategies to improve student achievement) whilst others may be engaged in focused classroom research activity (questioning technique, or cooperative groupwork). The scale of the intended impact is less significant than the quality of the knowledge deriving from the enquiry. A piece of classroom research, for example, can have equally powerful whole-school impact if the knowledge (about seating arrangements, starts and finishes of lessons – or whatever) is sufficiently significant and widely owned.

By 1997 we had incorporated into the model a group of students who were empowered to operate their own 'school improvement group' complementing and mirroring the style of the wider group. As the student voice dimension of our work evolved, we wanted more authentic and active involvement than 'passive voice'. Between a third and half the staff were, at this stage, involved any one year, focusing exclusively on enquiry and improvement issues.

The 1999/2000 model retains the concept of trios, but reverts to a focus specifically upon teaching and learning. Following a workshop with the whole staff, six areas of classroom practice were identified, and each of the trios has adopted one of these areas mandated by the whole staff. The first 'enquiry' task for each of the partnerships is to develop a powerful theoretical understanding of their particular teaching and learning focus – by researching the knowledge-base, observing classrooms, visiting other schools, or whatever. The trio will then practice and develop their skills in the classroom, providing in-house coaching for one another. The next phase will be to engage in action research with students to seek to validate the impact of this approach upon learning. Throughout this process the remainder of the staff (all staff not involved in one of the partnerships) will choose one of the areas, creating associate groups of about 15 staff for each partnership, who will follow the course of events, engage in workshops and generally become immersed and prepared. When (or if) the action research process validates the impact of the model, the associate staff will be asked to adopt the approach in their own classrooms and to be coached by the trio engaged in the original work.

This is a huge over-simplification of the model, but even described at this level it gives indications of the infrastructural and cultural changes that have evolved through the work of the various models. These would include:

- The opening up of classrooms and classroom practice and the legitimization of in-class coaching.
- The creation of a language to talk about teaching and school improvement.
- The integration of enquiry and professional development approaches.
- The value and authenticity of the student voice and the significance given to their perceptions as learners.
- The willingness of all staff to embrace the value of the development work emanating from the school improvement group.
- The ownership by the whole staff of the school improvement approach.
- The power of a sustained school improvement journey to win over those initially sceptical or even cynical.
- The expansion of leadership capacity.

The final example is taken from a paper by Lawrence Stenhouse (1979: 71–77) (reprinted by permission of Universitetsforlaget AS). He describes, in the first person singular, the fictionalized predicament of a teacher who turns to the research literature for advice on which teaching strategy to use.

I teach social studies in the form of a human issues programme covering such topics as the family, poverty, people and work, law and order, war and society, relations between the sexes. I wonder whether I should include race relations. A complicating factor is my style of teaching controversial issues to adolescent students. I set up discussions and use evidence such as newspapers, stories, pamphlets, photographs and films. I act as neutral chairman in those discussions, in order to encourage critical attitudes without taking sides. In short, I have been influenced by and am in the tradition of the English Humanities Curriculum Project (Stenhouse 1970).

I am very concerned that my teaching should contribute positively to race relations in my multiracial society, if that is possible. I wonder whether I should teach about race relations at all. If so, I wonder whether it is appropriate in this case to take the role of neutral chairman, even though this is a teaching convention and not a position professing personal neutrality. So I turn to a research report on 'Problems and Effects of Teaching about Race Relations' for enlightenment (Stenhouse *et al.* 1982, cited in Rudduck and Hopkins 1985).

Here I find that the project has monitored on a pre-test, post-test basis two different strategies of teaching about race relations, one in which the teacher is neutral (called strategy A), the other in which the teacher feels free to express, whenever he feels it appropriate, his committed stance against racism (called strategy B). Strategy A was conducted in 14 schools and strategy B in 16 schools. The samples are not true random samples because of problems of accessibility of schools and students, but I know something about this from my study of education at college (Campbell and Stanley 1963). Control groups have been gathered in the same schools as the experimental groups whenever this was possible, though this was not possible in all cases. I came across this table (see Table 2.2) of results on a scale purporting to measure general racism.

This seems to help me a good deal at first sight. My neutral strategy is strategy A. Attitudes in the strategy A group seem to improve and, though the improvement does not quite reach even the 0.05 level of significance, the control groups, left to general

Table 2.2 Scores on the General Racism Scale of the Bagley-Verma Test[a]

Teaching style	Experimental sample			Control sample			
	Pre-test mean (S.D.)	Post-test mean (S.D.)	Direction of shift and t-value for difference of means	Pre-test mean (S.D.)	Post-test mean (S.D.)	Direction of shift and t-value for difference of means	t-value for difference between the experimental and control groups
Strategy A							
Experimental (n = 258)	17.24 (10.05)	16.51 (10.25)	1.71				2.83**
Control (n = 124)				16.06 (9.66)	17.61 (10.49)	2.11*	
Strategy B							
Experimental (n = 359)	17.25 (9.61)	16.17 (9.78)	2.27				1.91
Control (n = 180)				17.42 (9.93)	17.87 (10.58)	0.72	

[a] A decrease in score represents a decrease in racism.
* P < 0.05; ** P < 0.01.

influences, deteriorate in attitude significantly and the comparison of experimental and control shows at least by one criterion a 0.01 level discrimination in favour of teaching about race relations by strategy A. Strategy B does not look markedly superior to strategy A, so I don't seem to need to change my teaching style. So it seems that research has helped me by enabling me to decide the right style in which to teach about race relations.

But, oh dear, here's a problem. On a later page the same data are presented in a different form to show the situation in individual schools and this seems to complicate the issue as shown in Table 2.3. Now, looking at this table, I personally feel that, given comment codes A, B or C, I certainly ought to proceed, given comment codes D and possibly E, I should proceed with great care, and given codes F and G, I might be better to give a lot more thought to the matter. In seven out of 12 schools, the result seems encouraging, in four schools results seem doubtful and in one of the 12 rather alarming. How do I know what category my school will fall into? This is really rather disturbing for my decision. Perhaps I should shift to strategy B. Let's look at the strategy B table (see Table 2.4).

Oh dear! This is no better. Here eight out of 15 schools are reassuring, three are doubtful and three are alarming. Strategy B seems no refuge.

Can it be that statistically significant discriminations between two treatments when presented through means and standard deviations can mask such a range of within-sample variance as this? It can indeed. In the psychostatistical research paradigm, the effects are not 'other things being equal'; they are 'by and large' or 'for the most part'. So doing one thing is only sometimes better than doing the other! This, apparently, depends on your school context or school environment or perhaps yourself or your pupils.

What I have to find out now is whether teaching about race relations by strategy A is good for my pupils in my school. However, that reminds me that I haven't looked at pupils as individuals, only as means and standard deviations. Suppose I took these data and looked at them in a way that depicted the fate of individuals. How about a histogram of change scores. There are, of course, problems with such scores but, bearing them in mind, I'll give it a go (see Figs 2.1 and 2.2).

My goodness, it looks as if the same teaching style and the same subject matter make some people worse as they make other people better. One man's meat is another man's poison. If I teach about race relations, some people get worse. But if I refuse to teach about race relations, even more people get worse. I suppose I should have

Table 2.3 Differences between pre- and post-test school means for the experimental and control groups on the General Racism (GR), Anti-Asian (AA) and Anti-Black (AB) Scales of the Bagley-Verma Test: Strategy A

1 School code	2 Experimental GR	3 Experimental AA	4 Experimental AB	5 Control GR	6 Control AA	7 Control AB	8 Comment code
03	-1.83	-0.35	-1.22	–	–	–	C
07**	1.58	0.54	0.31	-0.86	0.21	-0.71	G
09	-0.22	0.55	-0.90	2.11	1.45	1.09	A
10*	-0.63	-0.18	-1.54	–	–	–	C
13	-0.85	0.37	-1.29	-0.89	-0.56	-0.67	D
17	-2.50	-1.17	-1.78	–	–	–	C
18	1.70	2.40	0.90	6.63	4.38	3.75	B
19	0.37	-0.04	0.62	–	–	–	D
29	-3.42	-1.75	-1.67	2.0	0.87	-0.25	A
31**	-0.12	0.77	0.65	0.34	0.50	-1.16	D
32**	-1.61	-0.70	-0.83	-0.07	-0.77	-0.38	A
39*	1.20	-0.50	1.05	–	–	–	D
Mean of strategy A controls (individuals)				(1.30)	(0.83)	(0.49)	

* 5–25% non-white; ** over 25% non-white.

Table 2.4 Differences between pre- and post-test school means for the experimental and control groups on the General Racism (GR), Anti-Asian (AA) and Anti-Black (AB) Scales of the Bagley-Verma Test: Strategy B

1 School code	2 Experimental GR	3 Experimental AA	4 Experimental AB	5 Control GR	6 Control AA	7 Control AB	8 Comment code
01	-3.51	-1.60	-2.57	-1.75	1.43	-1.34	A
02	0.00	-0.67	-0.10	2.43	1.22	1.43	A
04*	1.04	0.10	0.24	–	–	–	E
05	-2.27	-0.34	-0.97	–	–	–	C
06*	-2.00	1.29	-1.30	0.55	0.34	-0.52	D
08	1.09	0.30	0.07	-5.40	-1.20	-2.33	G
09	-2.89	-0.22	-1.97	2.11	1.45	1.09	A
11	-1.58	-0.48	-0.53	–	–	–	C
14**	-0.33	0.39	0.91	–	–	–	D
15	-2.25	0.17	-1.42	–	–	–	C
20	-0.39	0.05	-0.22	-1.15	0.86	-1.43	F
21	-1.77	-1.32	-1.19	1.59	1.04	0.59	A
24*	0.19	0.37	0.60	4.93	1.07	1.65	B
30*	3.79	1.27	2.16	–	–	–	E
33	1.00	0.43	0.38	-0.83	0.83	-0.08	G
Mean of strategy B controls (individuals)				0.90	0.71	0.30	

* 5–25% non-white; ** over 25% non-white.

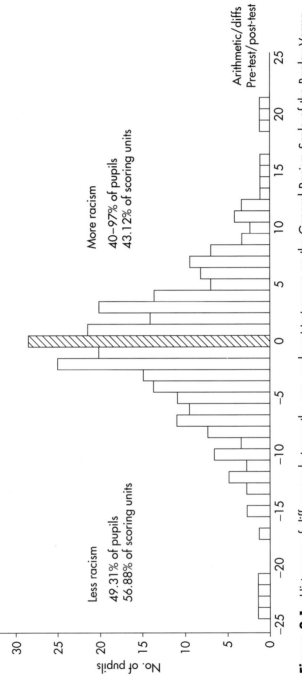

Figure 2.1 Histogram of differences between the pre- and post-test scores on the General Racism Scale of the Bagley-Verma Test: Strategy A experimental (n = 288).

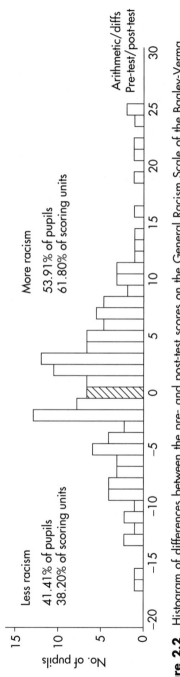

Figure 2.2 Histogram of differences between the pre- and post-test scores on the General Racism Scale of the Bagley-Verma Test: Strategy A control (*n* = 128).

thought of that anyway. I know that when I teach literature some people come not to like it, but I believe that even fewer would enjoy literature if I didn't introduce them to it all.

I need to steady myself. After all, engineers don't always build exactly the same bridge. Nor do chess players always play the same game. There must be ways of fitting action to situation and perhaps even to individuals in that situation.

I've clearly got to think things out for myself. Does this mean that research cannot help me? What was that piece in the paper by Cronbach they gave us in Ed. Psych? Here are my notes. And here it is:

When we give proper weight to local conditions, any generalization is a working hypothesis, not a conclusion.

(Cronbach 1975: 125)

That seems to mean that the results of research need testing in local conditions. What research gives me is most often not findings about all teaching but hypotheses about my teaching.

This is a bit of a shock, but it makes reasonable enough sense. And the hypotheses I've got are already of some use. I must test whether strategy A works well for me in my classroom, whether I can sustain its logic in practice and whether it is giving good results in attitudes. At the same time, I know that even in a good result some individuals may be deteriorating in attitude.

What I am going to do is this. I'm getting a student to come in and pre- and post-test my pupils and a control group in my school. But I'm also going to tape our sessions on race relations on a portable cassette-recorder. To do this, I have to tape other lessons too, so that I don't seem to be concentrating on race. I've started this. I'm explaining to the students that I'm doing a study of my own teaching and that this should help me to teach better. And I'm beginning to get them talking about how well my teaching and their learning goes.

Of course, there's a problem about how to handle the tapes. I played some at home and tried a Flanders Interaction Analysis (Flanders 1970) on them. It did tell me that I talked too much, but not a lot more. Then I tried the Humanities Curriculum Project analysis, which worked quite well because I was involved in discussion teaching. But I want to look at pupil behaviour as well as teacher behaviour. I'm beginning to ask myself whether I can develop a theory of individuals who cause me concern in class. I don't even need paper to do that. I can play cassettes in my car as I drive to and from work.

The more I come to study my own classroom, and my own school
as well, the more I come to understand why the research provides
case studies of classrooms. Comparing other people's experiences
with my own throws up all sorts of illuminating possibilities –
hypotheses, I mean.

At the end of this session, I'm going to try to set up a club in
the district for teacher-researchers. They have clubs for people
who tinker with motorcycles to get more performance from them,
so why not the same for teachers who are tinkering with their
teaching?

I'd like to set about testing Piaget. Most of his experiments are a
kind of teaching. And I have a feeling that if I work with a small
sample, like he did, I'll find out quite a lot for myself. I've got a
better laboratory than he had: it's a real classroom!

I'm not sure if I'm doing research. I am testing hypothesis by
experiment as systematically as a busy job allows.

The *Shorter Oxford English Dictionary* says that research is:
'Investigation, inquiry into things. Also, habitude of carrying out such
investigation.' Well, it is beginning to become a habit.

FURTHER READING

There are a number of sources for further examples of classroom research
by teachers. In *A Teacher's Guide to Action Research*, Jon Nixon (1981) presents
a series of descriptive accounts by teachers of a variety of classroom research projects. Extended illustrations of teacher research are given by
Michael Armstrong (1980) in *Closely Observed Children*. Classic examples of
classroom research in this tradition, although involving the participation of
an external researcher, are found in Smith and Geoffrey's (1968) *The Complexities of an Urban Classroom* and Stephen Rowland's (1984) *The Enquiring
Classroom*. Jean Rudduck and her colleagues (Hull *et al.* 1985; May and
Rudduck 1983; Rudduck 1981) have produced collections of teacher research accounts as a result of their funded research projects. During the
1980s, the Classroom Action Research Network (CARN), the Ford Teaching
Project, and the Teacher–Pupil Interaction and the Quality of Learning
(TIQL) project (Ebbutt and Elliott 1985; Elliott and Ebbutt 1985a,b) all
published accounts of their classroom research activities that were available
from the Centre for Applied Research in Education, University of East Anglia.
More recent collections of teacher research case studies are found in *Action
Research in Classrooms and Schools* (Hustler *et al.* 1986), which mainly focuses
on secondary schools, and Rosemary Webb's (1990) *Practitioner Research in
the Primary School*. Two other books that contain detailed examples of classroom research as well as descriptions of method and philosophical discussions

are *Collaborative Action Research* (Oja and Smulyan 1989) and Richard Winter's (1989) *Learning from Experience*.

Governmental interest in the 'teacher as researcher' concept has recently contributed considerable legitimacy to the movement. As a consequence, the research papers published by the Teacher Training Agency (TTA) now provide a rich and important source of classroom research case studies, as do the articles in *TOPIC* (published by the National Foundation for Educational Research) and *Improving Schools* (published by the Institute of Education, London). Homerton College publishes teachers' research accounts under the aegis of the Homerton – Schools' Research Circle.

CHAPTER 3

Why classroom research by teachers?

In asking the question, 'Why classroom research by teachers?', one is raising a whole series of issues around the topics of professionalism, classroom practice, the social control of teachers and the usefulness of educational research. Each of these issues provides a rationale for teacher research. For example, classroom research by teachers can be justified by references to professionalism because systematic self-study is a hallmark of those occupations that enjoy the label 'professional'. Unfortunately, the teacher's claim to professionalism sometimes falters at this definition. In this chapter, however, I will focus on three other themes that justify and, indeed, make imperative a concept of classroom research by teachers. The first is the link between classroom research by teachers and the establishing and refining of professional judgement. The second is making the focus of classroom research the curriculum and teaching learning. The third is the inappropriateness of the traditional research paradigm for helping teachers improve their teaching. I conclude the chapter with a reflection on the nature of classroom research itself.

'AUTONOMOUS IN PROFESSIONAL JUDGEMENT'

Lawrence Stenhouse (1984: 69) described the ideal role of the teacher like this:

> Good teachers are necessarily autonomous in professional judgement. They do not need to be told what to do. They are not professionally the dependants of researchers or superintendents, of innovators or supervisors. This does not mean that they do not welcome access to ideas created by other people at other places or in other times. Nor do they reject advice, consultancy or support.

> But they do know that ideas and people are not of much real use
> until they are digested to the point where they are subject to the
> teacher's own judgement in short, it is the task of all educational-
> ists outside the classroom to serve the teachers; for only teachers
> are in the position to create good teaching.

This is a very different image from the contemporary approach to schooling
that is based on the assumption that instructions issued from the top –
from the minister, the Director of education or headteacher – are put into
practice at the appropriate level lower down the organization. This approach to education tends to equate schools to factories which operate on
a rational input–output basis, with pupils as raw material, teachers as mechanics, the curriculum as the productive process and the school leaders as
factory managers.

This image of schooling stands in direct contrast to the aspirations
of the teacher research movement. John Elliott (in Nixon 1981: 1) has
observed that 'the teacher as researcher movement emanated from the
work and ideas of Lawrence Stenhouse'. Crucial to an understanding of
Stenhouse's intellectual position is, as we saw in Chapter 1, the notion of
emancipation (see Stenhouse 1983). In this context, emancipation refers to
the process involved in liberating teachers from a system of education that
denies individual dignity by returning to them some degree of self-worth
through the exercise of professional judgement.

In terms of curriculum and teaching, the path to emancipation involves reconceptualizing curriculum development as curriculum research,
and the linking of research to the art of teaching (Rudduck and Hopkins
1985). When viewed through this particular lens, centrally imposed curricula are in danger of becoming prescriptive blueprints that tend to inhibit
autonomy in teaching and learning. On the other hand, the process model
of curriculum, as described by Stenhouse (1975), is liberating or emancipatory because it encourages independence of thought and argument on the
part of the pupil, and experimentation and the use of judgement on the
part of the teacher. When teachers adopt this experimental approach to
their teaching, they are taking on an educational idea, cast in the form of a
curriculum proposal, and testing it out within their classrooms. As Stenhouse
(1975: 142) said:

> The crucial point is that the proposal is not to be regarded as an
> unqualified recommendation but rather as a provisional specifica-
> tion claiming no more than to be worth putting to the test of
> practice. Such proposals claim to be intelligent rather than correct.

The major consequence of doing this is that teachers take more control of
their professional lives. Not content to be told what to do or being uncertain

about what it is one is doing, teachers who engage in their own research are developing their professional judgement and are moving towards emancipation and autonomy. This idea is so central to the concept of the teacher as researcher, that I describe in Chapter 11 a series of practical ways in which teachers can refine their professional judgements. It is important to note that although this approach encourages new teaching strategies and implies a different way of viewing knowledge, it is not inimical to the idea of a National Curriculum or other curriculum guidelines, such as a National Literacy or Numeracy strategy.

CURRICULUM AND TEACHING AS THE FOCUS OF CLASSROOM RESEARCH

Successful implementation of any centralized innovation requires adaptation by teachers at the school level. It is not an either/or situation or a straight choice between 'top-down' or 'bottom-up' – it is a combination of both. As Denis Lawton (1989: 85) argues in his book *Education, Culture and the National Curriculum*:

> [we need] more curriculum development which is at least partly school-based. This is not to suggest that the centre–periphery or 'top-down' models of curriculum development are completely outmoded: it is a question of balance. It would be unreasonable to expect every school to develop its own curriculum from first principles, but it would be equally foolish to attempt to impose a detailed, uniform curriculum on every school, leaving no room for school-based development geared to specific local needs.

This balance is maintained through the professionalism of teachers. As Lawton (1989: 89) further comments:

> The increasing desire of teachers to be treated as professionals rather than as state functionaries, has encouraged a tendency to look for ways in which teachers could solve their own professional problems at a local level rather than react to more remote initiatives. Hence the emphasis on the school as the obvious location for curriculum renewal, the in service education of teachers, the evaluation of teaching and learning, and even educational research.

The crucial point that Lawton is making is that the claim of teaching to be a profession lies in the ability and opportunity for teachers to exercise their judgement over the critical tasks involved in their role, namely curriculum and teaching. Most centralized school systems prescribe what is to be taught to pupils, but require the teacher to put the curriculum into practice. At a very basic level, this involves the teacher in some form of 'translation' of the curriculum policy into schemes of work or lesson plans. More emphasis on research-based teaching would, I believe, result in better 'translations' of centralized curriculum into practice and in teachers who are more confident, flexible and autonomous.

A quarter of a century ago, Stenhouse made essentially the same point by suggesting that classroom research be used as a means of testing curriculum ideas. The context of that proposal is worth reproducing in full (Stenhouse 1975: 142–3):

> I have argued that educational ideas expressed in books are not easily taken into possession by teachers, whereas the expression of ideas as curricular specifications exposes them to testing by teachers and hence establishes an equality of discourse between the proposer and those who assess the proposal. There is, of course, no implication as to the origins of the proposal or hypotheses being tested. The originator may be a classroom teacher, a policy-maker or an educational research worker. The crucial point is that the proposal is not to be regarded as an unqualified recommendation but rather as a provisional specification claiming no more than to be worth putting to the test of practice. Such proposals claim to be intelligent rather than correct.
>
> I have identified a curriculum as a particular form of specification about the practice of teaching and not as a package of materials of a syllabus of ground to be covered. It is a way of translating any educational idea into a hypothesis testable in practice. It invites critical testing rather than acceptance.
>
> I have reached towards a research design based upon these ideas, implying that a curriculum is a means of studying the problems and effects of implementing any defined line of teaching.
>
> The uniqueness of each classroom setting implies that any proposal – even at school level – needs to be tested and verified and adapted by each teacher in his own classroom. The ideal is that the curricular specification should feed a teacher's personal research and development programme through which he is progressively increasing his understanding of his own work and hence bettering his teaching.
>
> To summarise the implications of this position, all well-founded curriculum research and development, whether the work of an individual teacher, of a school, or of a group working in a teachers' centre or of a group working within the co-ordinating framework of a national project, is based on the study of classrooms. It thus rests on the work of teachers.

Here Stenhouse is linking classroom research by teachers firmly to the curriculum and teaching. This is an important point that may have been lost in all the talk about the gathering and analysis of data. Teacher research is not an end in itself, but is inextricably linked to curriculum change and the adoption of new teaching strategies. It is also at this point that teaching becomes a profession.

PROBLEMS IN TRADITIONAL APPROACHES

Perhaps the most unfortunate aspect of traditional educational research is that it is extremely difficult to apply its findings to classroom practice. The final case study in Chapter 2 is a good illustration of this. In a quandary about which teaching strategy to use, the fictionalized teacher went to the research literature for guidance. His subsequent experience was as frustrating as it was predictable, because the literature contains few unequivocal signposts for action. This dilemma is widespread: teachers quite rightly (in most cases) regard educational research as something irrelevant to their lives and see little interaction between the world of the educational researcher and the world of the teacher.

Arthur Bolster (1983: 295) asked the question, 'Why has research on teaching had so little influence on practice?', and his response to the question is worth quoting:

> The major reason, in my opinion, is that most such research, especially that emanating from top-ranked schools of education, construes teaching from a theoretical perspective that is incompatible with the perspective teachers must employ in thinking about their work. In other words, researchers and school teachers adopt radically different sets of assumptions about how to conceptualize the teaching process. As a result, the conclusions of much formal research on teaching appear irrelevant to classroom teachers – not necessarily wrong, just not very sensible or useful. If researchers are to generate knowledge that is likely to affect classroom practice, they must construe their inquiries in ways that are much more compatible with teachers' perspectives.

Most researchers, when they enter classrooms, bring with them perspectives derived from academic disciplines. Their view of how knowledge evolves and how it is determined are firmly established by their formal training. The world view that guides researchers' actions is consequently at odds with that of teachers. The teacher derives his or her knowledge of teaching from continual participation in situational decision making and the classroom culture in which they and their pupils live out their daily lives. So one reason why traditional educational research is of little use to teachers is because of the differing conceptions of teaching held by teachers and researchers. But there are other problems.

Research in education is usually carried out within the psycho-statistical research paradigm. This implies tightly controlled experimentation and the testing of hypotheses by assessing the effectiveness of a treatment across randomly selected groups through the use of statistical analysis. This approach is based on the agricultural research designs of R.A. Fisher (1966) in the 1930s. At that time, educationalists, desiring to link research to action, began to utilize the very successful 'agricultural–botany' designs of Fisher in educational settings. This has continued (and increased) down to the present day as can be seen by the myriad of postgraduate theses that use this research design. The basic idea underlying Fisher's designs is that experiments are conducted on samples, usually divided into a control and an experimental group, with the results generalized to the target popula-tion. The point is that samples are randomly drawn and are consequently representative of that target population.

Stenhouse (1979) describes Fisher's approach like this:

> The strength of Fisher's paradigm is the recognition of random sampling, in which a sample is drawn such that each member of the target population has an equal chance of being included in the sample because it is a device of chance . . .
>
> In Fisher's agricultural setting, the hypotheses were not derived from scientific theory . . . They were hypotheses regarding the rel-ative effectiveness of alternative procedures, and the criteria of effectiveness was gross crop yield.
>
> The result of an experiment of this kind is an estimate of the probability that – other things being equal – a particular seed strain or fertilizer or amount of watering will result in a higher gross yield than an alternative against which it has been tested . . . It is in applying experimental methods to teaching and curriculum evalu-ation in the schools that researchers have used the Fisherian model. The assumption is that one teaching procedure or curriculum can be tested against alternatives as a seed strain or fertilizer can in agriculture, i.e. procedures can be tested against yield without a real theoretical framework.

This approach to educational research is problematic, particularly if its results are to be applied to classrooms. First, it is extraordinarily difficult to draw random samples in educational settings (e.g. a random sample of schools, pupils and teachers would have to be drawn separately). Second, there are a myriad of contextual variables operating on schools and classrooms (e.g. community culture, teacher personality, school ethos, socio-economic background, etc.) that would affect the results. Third, it is difficult to establish criteria for effective classroom or school performance. Even if one could resolve these difficulties, there are, as Stenhouse (1979) points out, two deeper problems that relate to the nature of educational activity.

First, the 'agricultural–botany' paradigm is based on measures of gross yield (i.e. how much produce can be gathered in total from a section of land). That is an inappropriate measure for education. As teachers, we are concerned with the individual progress of students rather than with aggregated scores from the class or the school. Our emphasis is on varying teaching methods to suit individual pupils in order to help them achieve to the limit of their potential. Stenhouse (1979: 79) puts the paradox like this:

> The teacher is like a gardener who treats different plants differently, and not like a large scale farmer who administers standardised treatments to as near as possible standardised plants.

The second deeper problem relates to meaningful action. The teacher–pupil or pupil–pupil interactions that result in effective learning are not so much the consequence of a standardized teaching method but the result of both teachers and pupils engaging in meaningful action. And meaningful action cannot be standardized by control or sample. This is a similar argument to the one commonly used against those who overrate the utility of behavioural objectives. Behavioural objectives provide an excellent means for the teaching of skills or evaluating rote learning, but they tend to be counter-productive with more complex and sophisticated content areas. In the instance of rote learning, one can accept the parallel with standardized treatments, but not so easily with poetry appreciation. Here pupil response is the result of individual negotiation with the subject, mediated through and by the teacher – namely, a form of meaningful action. In this case, education as induction into knowledge is, as Stenhouse (1975: 82) memorably points out, 'successful to the extent that it makes the behavioural outcomes of pupils unpredictable' and, therefore, not generalizable. The implications of this line of thinking for teacher-researchers is to encourage them to look outside the psycho-statistical paradigm for their research procedures.

To summarize, I have made two points in arguing that the traditional approach to educational research is not of much use to teachers. The first point is that teachers and researchers do not conceptualize teaching in the same way. They live in different intellectual worlds and so their meanings rarely connect. Second, the usual form of educational research, the psycho-statistical or agricultural–botany paradigm, has severe limitations as a method of construing and making sense of classroom reality. For these two reasons, teachers and those concerned with understanding classroom life have increasingly adopted different approaches to classroom research.

THE NATURE OF CLASSROOM RESEARCH

So far in this chapter I have been arguing for classroom research by teachers on three grounds: the first being its role in refining professional judgement; the second, being its focus on the key professional activities of teachers; and third, the inadequacy of existing research paradigms for teacher researchers. There is, however, a further issue on which to reflect when discussing the importance of classroom research: the nature of the research activity itself. This is an issue that has vexed teacher-researchers and those that comment on it for some time.

As a precursor to the discussion, let me quote from Ebbutt (1985: 157):

> If action research is to be considered legitimately as research, the participants in it must, it seems to me, be prepared to produce written reports of their activities.
>
> Moreover these reports ought to be available to some form of public critique. I would go as far as to say that if this condition is not satisfied by participants then no matter how personally and professionally valuable the exercise is in which they are engaged, it is not action research.

While I would agree with Ebbutt's call for written reports and critique, particularly by other teacher-researchers, I disagree with the implication that unless the research is published it is not research. It seems to me that many current commentators on classroom research have a misplaced conception of what research actually is. Michael Armstrong (1982) exemplified this position well:

> I have grown impatient with the concept of 'research'. In the context of a study of education it has acquired too narrow a connotation especially in regard to criteria for rigour, evidence and validity. I prefer the word 'enquiry' . . . The form of enquiry which I have in mind is grounded in the experience of teaching and in particular in that practice of sustained observation which is inseparable from good teaching . . .

Armstrong seems to be saying, 'Let's call it enquiry and let's keep it in the classroom and then we won't need to tangle with such questions as what counts as research.' Hull *et al.* (1985) complicate this position even further. They appear to say, 'Let's call what Armstrong does self-monitoring "an investigation of one's own practice in private" but let's recognize that there is also teacher research.' They argue that teacher research (Hull *et al.* 1985):

... must feed a tradition – from which individual researchers can derive support. In this way it is quite different from the activity which has been called 'self-monitoring' where a teacher uses some of the data-gathering techniques developed by researchers to record instances of their own practice as a basis for reflection. The self-monitoring teacher makes no claims to be methodologically reflexive. He or she does not undertake responsibility either to introduce 'system' into the investigations or make accounts of the studies available to other teachers. Self-monitoring is essentially a privatised encounter between a practitioner and practice. As such it has immense value. We conceive teacher research however, as potentially the root of a tradition of enquiry into educational processes which might stand alongside the academic tradition as an alternative body of knowledge rooted firmly in practice.

These claims are to me both confused and pedantic. The dichotomy that Armstrong and Hull and their co-workers point to is just not there. Armstrong's Closely Observed Children (1980) is one of the best teacher research studies. It is sensitive, insightful and profound; it is research at a high level of sophistication, imagination and rigour. Armstrong is doing teacher research in general, and himself in particular, a grave disservice to claim otherwise. One can readily appreciate Armstrong's 'impatience with the concept of research' but to call it something else is not to change anything. What he is impatient of is narrowly defined psycho-statistical research that has little to say to teachers, not research *per se*.

Research, enquiry and self-monitoring are all aspects of a similar activity because they all require systematic, self-conscious and rigorous reflection to be of any value. The problem is that psychological research, with its emphasis on statistical manipulation, has captured the educational imagination to such an extent that most people cannot think of research in any other terms. But criteria, such as validity or internal consistency, are necessary if teacher researchers are to escape the sentimental anecdote that often replaces statistical research designs in education, and gives teacher research such a bad name. Enquiry, self-monitoring and teacher research need to establish standards and criteria that are applicable to their area of activity, rather than assume (and then reject) criteria designed for different procedures.

Teacher research, like enquiry and self-monitoring, is a form of research. These forms may be presented to different audiences and formulated in different ways, but all are attempts to create meaning out of complex situations. And the meaning is only valid when it is subject to certain methodological standards. It is naive to argue that just because we call what we do enquiry or self-monitoring instead of research we can escape the demand for valid judgement. That is throwing the baby out with the bath water. It is equally incorrect to assume that just because we engage in research, we have to follow the criteria of the psycho-statistical research paradigm. These criteria are inappropriate and other more suitable methods, like the ones discussed in subsequent chapters, have to be sought.

There are two important points to be drawn from this discussion. The first is that classroom research by teachers is a valid form of research because it results in hypotheses generated through a rigorous process of enquiry and grounded in the data to which they apply. This meets contemporary criteria for research. In the article to which I have already referred, Ebbutt (1985: 157) cites:

> Shulman's conception of what counts as research, that it is 'a family of methods which share the characteristics of disciplined inquiry' . . .
>
> 1 arguments and evidence can be examined
> 2 not dependent solely on eloquence or surface plausibility
> 3 avoids sources of error when possible and discusses margin for possible errors in conclusion
> 4 can be speculative, free wheeling and inventive.

This, it seems to me, is an accurate description of classroom research as it is being described in this book.

The second point is that it is important for teacher-researchers to open up their work to critique and, if possible, to publish it. It is pleasing in this respect to see the publication of teacher research reports in England by the Teacher Training Agency, the Department for Education and Skills and the National College for School Leadership. The importance of public critique in classroom research is that it encourages a discourse among teachers, that is research-oriented and committed to action and the improvement of practice. It is the sharing of our experiences and the social and intellectual benefits that emanate from it, not the meeting of some abstract academic criteria, that provide the logic for publication and critique in classroom research. But the important point is that the mere fact of publication cannot be a judgement on the nature of the process that led (or did not lead) to publication.

In this section, I have argued strenuously against those who claim that teacher research is not really research. Their position is untenable because: (1) it is a capitulation in the face of the norms of traditional research; (2) it devalues the quality of teacher-research efforts; and (3) it avoids the necessity of establishing a rigorous methodology for classroom research. For these reasons I am calling the form of research in which teachers do research in their own classrooms for the purpose of improving practice, teacher research. The phrase, teacher research, has the advantage of being simple and identifies the major actor and the process involved. It is in this sense and with this aspiration that the terms 'classroom research by teachers', 'teacher-based research' and the 'teacher-researcher' are used in this book. It is the description of such an approach to classroom research that provides the substance of the following chapter.

FURTHER READING

The notion of professionalism used in this chapter comprises a major theme in two of Lawrence Stenhouse's books: *An Introduction to Curriculum Research and Development* (1975) and *Authority, Education and Emancipation* (1983). An important discussion of the historical background to the nature of teacher professionalism is included in Dan Lortie's (1975) *School Teacher*. An excellent wide-ranging discussion of the practical implications of professionalism is found in Donald Schön's (1991) *The Reflective Practitioner*. A more contemporary discussion of reflective professionalism in teaching is found in the contributions to *Quality in Teaching*, edited by Wilf Carr (1989). For a more detailed exposition of Stenhouse's critique of the traditional approach to educational research, see *Research as a Basis for Teaching* (Rudduck and Hopkins 1985). An entertaining and comprehensive review of the arguments against traditional educational research as well as an alternative approach is found in *Beyond the Numbers Game* (Hamilton *et al.* 1977). These arguments are also well rehearsed in Winter's (1989) *Learning from Experience*, Carr and Kemmis's (1986) *Becoming Critical* and Elliott's (1991) *Action Research for Educational Change*. A broader perspective on this 'alternative approach' to educational research is found in texts such as Lincoln and Guba's (1985) *Naturalistic Inquiry*, Sara Delamont's (1992) witty and perceptive *Fieldwork in Educational Settings* and Colin Robson's (1993) *Real World Research*.

CHAPTER 4

Action research and classroom research by teachers

In the previous chapter, I outlined a series of problems associated with the traditional approach to educational research that limits its usefulness for teachers who wish to improve their practice. There are, however, at least two other research traditions to which teachers can turn. One tradition is associated with the work of sociologists and anthropologists. Social anthropological, ethnographic, phenomenological, naturalistic and illuminative research are examples of these research approaches. These are long words that describe essentially the same approach – one that attempts to understand a social situation and to derive hypotheses from that effort of appreciation. The procedures that such social scientists have developed for analysing fieldwork data are used in this book as a guide for making sense of classroom data. They are described in some detail in Chapter 9.

The other research tradition that stands in contrast to the psycho-statistical paradigm and has a strong link with contemporary social science research is the method known as action research. In recent years, teacher-researchers have adopted the label 'action research' to describe their particular approach to classroom research. In this chapter, I describe and critique this application of action research, and from the discussion propose six criteria for classroom research by teachers.

ACTION RESEARCH

Action research combines a substantive act with a research procedure; it is action disciplined by enquiry, a personal attempt at understanding while engaged in a process of improvement and reform.

Here are four definitions of action research. The first is by Robert Rapoport (1970), who says that action research:

aims to contribute both to the practical concerns of people in an immediate problematic situation and to the goals of social science by joint collaboration within a mutually acceptable ethical framework.

The second is by Stephen Kemmis (1983), who writes:

> Action research is a form of self-reflective enquiry undertaken by participants in social (including educational) situations in order to improve the rationality and justice of (a) their own social or educational practices, (b) their understanding of these practices, and (c) the situations in which the practices are carried out. It is most rationally empowering when undertaken by participants collaboratively, though it is often undertaken by individuals, and sometimes in cooperation with 'outsiders'. In education, action research has been employed in school-based curriculum development, professional development, school improvement programs, and systems planning and policy development.

The third is taken from a paper by Dave Ebbutt (1985), who not only gives a definition of his own, but also quotes from Kemmis. He writes that action research:

> is about the systematic study of attempts to improve educational practice by groups of participants by means of their own practical actions and by means of their own reflection upon the effects of those actions.
> Put simply action research is the way groups of people can organise the conditions under which they can learn from their own experience. (Kemmis)
> Action research is trying out an idea in practice with a view to improving or changing something, trying to have a real effect on the situation. (Kemmis)

The fourth is from John Elliott (1991: 69):

> Action-research might be defined as *'the study of a social situation with a view to improving the quality of action within it'*. It aims to feed practical judgement in concrete situations, and the validity of the 'theories' or hypotheses it generates depends not so much on 'scientific' tests of truth, as on their usefulness in helping people to act more intelligently and skilfully. In action-research 'theories' are

not validated independently and then applied to practice. They are validated through practice.

The development of the idea of action research is generally attributed to Kurt Lewin, who in the immediate post-war period used it as a methodology for intervening in and researching the major social problems of the day. Lewin maintained that through action research advances in theory and needed social changes might simultaneously be achieved. Action research, according to Lewin, 'consisted in analysis, fact-finding, conceptualisation, planning execution, more fact-finding or evaluation; and then a repetition of this whole circle of activities; indeed a spiral of such circles' (quoted in Kemmis 1988: 13).

Lewin's ideas on action research were almost immediately applied to education, as well as social science more generally. It was the work of Stephen Corey at Teacher's College, Columbia University, however – in particular, his book *Action Research to Improve School Practice* (1953) – that spread the word about action research into 'main stream' American education.

More recently, action research has been seen as a methodology through which the aspirations of critical theory, which itself is regarded as an increasingly important trend in the philosophy of social science and the study of education, might be realized. Critical theory builds on the work of Marx, Freud and the traditions of the 'Frankfurt School' of philosophy, in particular the writings of Jurgen Habermas. Unfortunately, the outstanding characteristic of critical theory is its unintelligibility! This is a great pity as well as a paradox, because the central purpose of critical theory is emancipation – enabling people to take control and direction over their own lives. There are now, however, a number of books that admirably 'translate' critical theory and explore its educational implications. In one of them, Rex Gibson (1986: 5–6) describes the central characteristic of critical theory like this:

> Critical theory acknowledges the sense of frustration and powerlessness that many feel as they see their personal destinies out of their control, and in the hands of (often unknown) others . . . Critical theory attempts to reveal those factors which prevent groups and individuals taking control of, or even influencing, those decisions which crucially affect their lives . . . In the exploration of the nature and limits of power, authority and freedom, critical theory claims to afford insight into how greater degrees of autonomy could be available.
>
> This characteristic marks out critical theory's true distinctiveness: its claim to be *emancipatory*. Not only does it provide enlightenment (deeper awareness of your true interests); more than that (indeed, because of that), it can set you free. Unlike scientific theory, it claims to provide guidance as to what to do.

If this all sounds too good to be true, Gibson (1986: 6) goes on to warn us that:

> There are clearly immense problems attaching to a theory which not only argues that it reveals the world more clearly, but also asserts that it can be used to change the world, to liberate from inequalities and unfair restrictions.

Obviously, neither critical theory nor action research are panaceas and they should not be regarded as such. We shall continue to see in this book, however, that their practical applications do provide a rationale and method for teachers who wish to take more control of their professional (and personal) lives.

From even this brief description, it can be seen how the method of action research with its twin emphasis on committed action and reflection is particularly suited to putting into practice such an emancipatory philosophy. There is also a pleasing symmetry between this more abstract discussion and the practical educational philosophy of Lawrence Stenhouse, and those who have followed his lead, as we see in the following section.

MODELS OF ACTION RESEARCH

The combination of the action and the research components has a powerful appeal for teachers. In the UK, Lawrence Stenhouse was quick to point to the connection between action research and his concept of the teacher as researcher. Later, John Elliott popularized action research as a method for teachers doing research in their own classrooms through the Ford Teaching Project, and established the Classroom Action Research Network.

Subsequently, Stephen Kemmis refined and formalized the concept of action research and how it applies to education. His articles on action research (Kemmis 1983, 1988) are a useful review of how educational action research has developed from the work of Lewin and established its own character. Of more interest to us here is his 'Action Research Planner' (Kemmis and McTaggart 1988), where a sequential programme for teachers intending to engage in action research is outlined in some detail. He summarizes his approach to action research in the model shown in Fig. 4.1.

John Elliott was quick to take up Kemmis's schema of the action research spiral and he, too, produced a similar but more elaborate model, as seen in Fig. 4.2. Elliott (1991: 70) summarizes Kemmis's approach and then outlines his elaborations like this:

> Although I think Kemmis' model is an excellent basis for starting to think about what action research involves, it can allow those

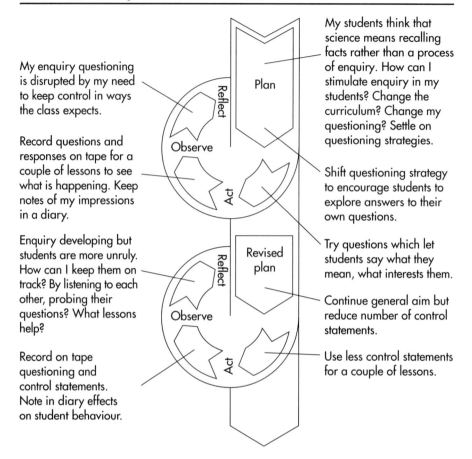

My students think that science means recalling facts rather than a process of enquiry. How can I stimulate enquiry in my students? Change the curriculum? Change my questioning? Settle on questioning strategies.

My enquiry questioning is disrupted by my need to keep control in ways the class expects.

Record questions and responses on tape for a couple of lessons to see what is happening. Keep notes of my impressions in a diary.

Shift questioning strategy to encourage students to explore answers to their own questions.

Enquiry developing but students are more unruly. How can I keep them on track? By listening to each other, probing their questions? What lessons help?

Try questions which let students say what they mean, what interests them.

Continue general aim but reduce number of control statements.

Record on tape questioning and control statements. Note in diary effects on student behaviour.

Use less control statements for a couple of lessons.

Figure 4.1 The 'action research spiral' (based on Kemmis and McTaggart 1988: 14).

who use it to assume that 'The General Idea' can be fixed in advance, that 'Reconnaissance' is merely fact-finding and that 'Implementation' is a fairly straightforward process. But I would argue that:

'The General Idea' should be allowed to shift.

'Reconnaissance' should involve analysis as well as fact-finding, and should constantly recur in the spiral of activities, rather than occur only at the beginning.

'Implementation' of an action-step is not always easy, and one should not proceed to evaluate the effects of an action until one has monitored the extent to which it has been implemented.

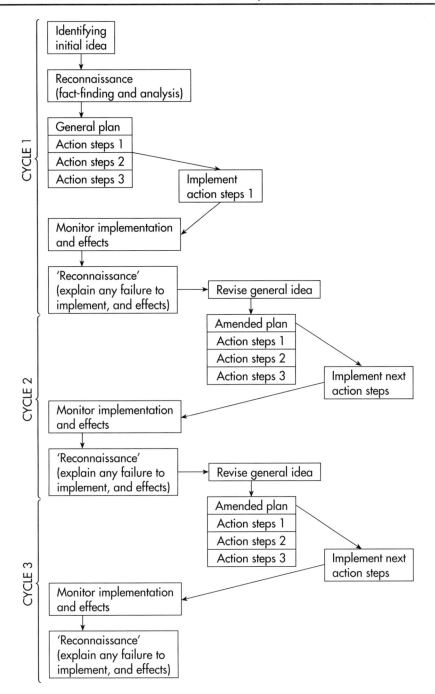

Figure 4.2 Elliott's action research model (from Elliott 1991: 71).

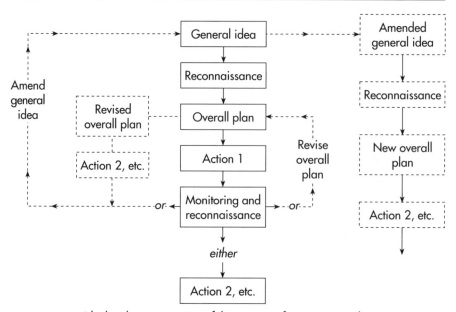

Idealized representation of the process of action research

Figure 4.3 Ebbutt's model.

Dave Ebbutt (1985), a colleague of Elliott, provides us with another variation on Kemmis's model and makes these comments about it:

> It seems clear to me that Elliott is wrong in one respect, in suggest-
> ing that Kemmis equates reconnaissance with fact finding only.
> The Kemmis diagram clearly shows reconnaissance to comprise
> discussing, negotiating, exploring opportunities, assessing possibili-
> ties and examining constraints – in short there are elements of
> analysis in the Kemmis notion of reconnaissance. Nevertheless I
> suggest that the thrust of Elliott's three statements is an attempt on
> the part of a person experienced in directing action research projects
> to recapture some of the 'messiness' of the action-research cycle
> which the Kemmis version tends to gloss.

But Ebbutt (1985) claims that the spiral is not the most useful metaphor.
Instead, the most:

> appropriate way to conceive of the process of action research is to
> think of it as comprising of a series of successive cycles, each incor-
> porating the possibility for the feedback of information within and
> between cycles. Such a description is not nearly so neat as conceiving
> of the process as a spiral, neither does it lend itself quite so tidily to

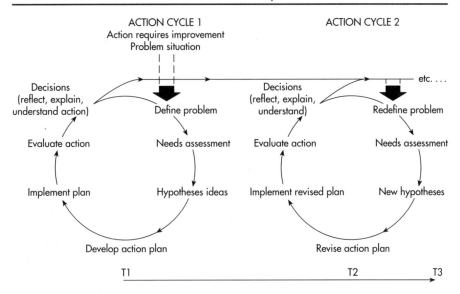

Figure 4.4 McKernan's action research model (from McKernan 1996: 29).

a diagrammatic representation. In my view the idealized process of educational action research can be more appropriately represented like this: [as shown in Fig. 4.3]

A number of other similar models have recently been developed, most of which build on Lewin's original idea or Kemmis's interpretation of it. For example, James McKernan (1996) has suggested a 'time process' model (see Fig. 4.4) which emphasizes the importance of not allowing an action research 'problem' to become too rigidly fixed in time, and of rational problem solving and democratic ownership by the community of researchers.

My purpose in presenting these four practical models of action research is twofold. First, I intend to provide an overview of action research to help the reader gain an understanding of the whole process. Second, it is to demonstrate that despite the proliferation of eponymous 'models', they do, in fact, share more similarities than differences. There is a high degree of consensus among those who write on the subject about overall method and purpose. There are, however, some problems inherent in these models and to these I now turn.

CRITIQUE OF EDUCATIONAL ACTION RESEARCH

There are three main areas of concern that I have with the action research models developed by Kemmis, Elliott, Ebbutt, McKernan and others. Although this is not the place for a thoroughgoing critique, a brief discussion of these concerns is necessary because the problems may lead teacher-researchers into possible confusion. Also, the critique will help explain the form and structure of the rest of the book.

My first concern is that there may be a misunderstanding of the nature of Lewinian action research. As I mentioned earlier, the term action research was coined as a useful label to describe what teacher-researchers were doing. Recently, much energy has been devoted to setting out the intellectual basis for action research as it derived from Lewin. Lewin's conception of action research is, however, very different in some respects to what goes on in the name of teacher research. Lewin's concept of action research was (1) as an externally initiated intervention designed to assist a client system, (2) functionalist in orientation and (3) prescriptive in practice. None of these features apply to what I assume to be the nature of classroom research by teachers which is characterized by its practitioner, problem solving, and eclectic orientation.

We should take care that what began as a useful label to describe teacher research for professional development purposes does not assume a different character as a result of a quest for intellectual credibility.

My second concern relates to the specification of process in the action research models. There are three interrelated points. The first is that the tight specification of process steps and cycles may trap teachers within a framework which they may come to depend on and which will, consequently, inhibit independent action. The original purpose of teacher research was to free teachers from the constraints of prespecified research designs. It is useful to have a guide for action; my concern is when it becomes, or appears to become, prescriptive. Second, the models outline a process rather than a technology. They delineate a sequence of stages, but say little about the 'what' and the 'how' within these stages. Third, the models may appear daunting and confusing to practitioners. Ebbutt himself admits that Elliott's framework tends to 'mystification'.

Unfortunately, models and frameworks cannot mirror reality: they are one individual's interpretation of reality. Consequently, they impose upon the user a prespecified analysis of a process that the user may quite rightly interpret differently. At best, they provide a starting point, an initial guide to action. At worst, they trap the practitioners within a set of assumptions that bear little relationship to their reality and, consequently, constrain their freedom of action.

The line between specifying principles of procedure that encourage informed action, and prescribing activities that determine behaviour and limit outcomes, is a fine one indeed. There is a real danger that teacher research will assume the character of the objectives model, which 'is like a site-plan simplified so that people know exactly where to dig their trenches without having to know why' (Stenhouse 1980). To use Jean Rudduck's felicitous phrase, it seems that already 'the elusive butterfly of teacher research has been caught and pinned'.

My third concern is a semantic one. There is a tendency for some 'action researchers' to overuse words and phrases like *'problem'*, *'improve'*, *'needs assessment'* and so on. This could give the impression that action research is a deficit model of professional development. 'Something is wrong, so do this to make it better.' I know that this is not the intention, and I am as guilty of this as anyone in this regard, but it does behove all of us to talk (and write) about classroom research in as positive a way as we can. At the present time, the teaching profession in the UK is suffering from low morale largely as a result of ill-informed public and political criticism. Action research is one way of restoring and enhancing professional confidence.

These concerns notwithstanding, the importance of action research is not to be underestimated. Action research provides teachers with a more appropriate alternative to traditional research designs and one that is, in aspiration at least, emancipatory. We must, however, be aware of the problems associated with too prescriptive a framework for action and the values that are embedded within it. Consequently, I tend to use terms like 'classroom research by teachers' rather than action research. This is not a fundamental point of difference with those colleagues I have cited earlier. It does, however, serve to emphasize the importance of the acquisition of skills and techniques that become part of a teacher's repertoire and which are then subject to the exercise of his or her professional judgement.

CLASSROOM RESEARCH BY TEACHERS

My preference for the phrase 'classroom research by teachers' rather than 'action research' will not lead me to produce an alternative step-by-step model. Instead, I will present a series of methods and techniques that teachers can use in their classroom research efforts. In particular, I will discuss:

1 Ways in which classroom research projects can be identified and initiated (Chapter 5).
2 Principles and methods of classroom observation and of other ways of gathering data on classroom behaviours (Chapters 6–8).
3 Ways of interpreting, analysing and reporting the data gathered from classroom research (Chapter 9).
4 Ways in which the research process can be linked to a focus on teaching and learning (Chapter 10).
5 Ways in which classroom research methods can link to development planning and other school improvement initiatives (Chapter 11).

6 How staff development activities and networking can support teacher and school development (Chapter 12).

My purpose in tackling classroom research in this way is to give teachers an introduction to the variety of methods available to them as a means of extending their repertoire of professional practices and of encouraging flexibility in professional development. These are methods and approaches that teachers can put into use, that will empower them, and make them increasingly competent and 'autonomous in professional judgement'.

CRITERIA FOR CLASSROOM RESEARCH BY TEACHERS

The essence of what I am advocating is the development of a teacher's professional expertise and judgement. Although many teachers are in broad agreement with this general aim, some are quite rightly concerned about how far involvement in classroom research activity will impinge upon their teaching and on their personal time. Concerns are also raised as to the utilitarian or practical value of classroom research. With these concerns in mind, let me suggest the following six principles for classroom research by teachers.

The first is that the teacher's primary job is to teach, and any research method should not interfere with or disrupt the teaching commitment. This rule of thumb should serve to quell immediate concerns, but it also points to certain ethical considerations. In some instances, it may be inevitable that the adoption of a new and barely internalized teaching strategy is initially less effective than the way one previously taught. Is it ethical, therefore, some may ask, for a teacher to subject students to an inferior performance when the original behaviour was perfectly adequate? These are questions which ultimately can only be answered by the individuals involved. For my part, I am prepared to stand behind the teacher's judgement, particularly if the teachers involved are so concerned about improving the teaching and the learning experience of their students that they have broken the mould and are experimenting with new models. In becoming a teacher-researcher, the individual teacher is deliberately and consciously expanding his or her role to include a professional element. It is almost inconceivable, then, that he or she would do this and at the same time ignore the primacy of the teaching/learning process.

The second criterion is that the method of data collection must not be too demanding on the teacher's time. As a corollary, the teacher needs to be certain about the data collection technique before using it. The reasons for this are obvious. Teachers already consider themselves overworked and there are continuing demands for increased preparation and professional development time. It is naive to assume that the adoption of a research role will make no inroads on a teacher's private time. This can be reduced, however, by judicious use of specific data collection techniques, and the utilization of easily analysed diagnostic methods. For example, the tape-recorder is widely regarded as a very useful tool for the classroom researcher. It is, however, extremely expensive to use both in terms of time and money. It takes approximately 50 per cent longer to listen to a tape than to make it, and on top of that transcription (which is necessary if full use is to be made of the method) is both time-consuming and expensive. Given this, it is advisable to use another method for broad spectrum diagnosis and reserve such intensive techniques for specific and finely focused enquiries. A number of techniques for classroom observation are discussed in Chapter 7 and a taxonomy of data collection techniques is presented in Chapter 8.

The third principle is perhaps the most contentious. The methodology employed must be reliable enough to allow teachers to formulate hypotheses confidently and develop strategies applicable to their classroom situation. Traditional researchers hold a poor opinion of action research. In many cases, that opinion is well-founded, particularly if it is based on individual pieces of research. It behoves all researchers, be they psycho-statisticians engaged in large-scale research or a primary teacher testing Piaget's theoretical hypotheses, to be rigorous about their methodology. It is no excuse at all to claim that rigour is unnecessary because the research is practitioner-oriented, small-scale or used solely to improve individual practice. If a change in teaching strategy is to be made, then that decision needs to be based on reliable data. These issues form the substance of Chapter 8.

The fourth criterion is that the research focus undertaken by the teacher should be one to which he or she is committed. Although this sounds self-evident, it is difficult enough, given all the pressures on a teacher's time, to sustain energy in a project even if it is intrinsically interesting and important to the teacher's professional activities. As a corollary, the problem must in fact be a problem; that is, the problem must be capable of solution, else by definition it is not a problem. If a teacher chooses a topic that is too complex or amorphous, then frustration and disillusionment will soon set in.

The fifth criterion refers to the need for teacher-researchers to pay close attention to the ethical procedures surrounding their work. Ethical standards for classroom researchers were worked out during the 1970s and 1980s by researchers associated with the Centre for Applied Research in Education (e.g. MacDonald and Walker 1974; Simons 1982, 1987). A summary of ethical procedures for teacher-researchers can be found in the Appendix.

The sixth criterion is that as far as possible classroom research should adopt a 'classroom exceeding' perspective. What I mean by this is that all members of a school community actively build and share a common vision of their main purpose. Teachers are now increasingly relating the teaching and learning focus of their classroom research efforts to whole school priorities through the use of classroom observation techniques. They adapt educational ideas and policies to suit their own context and professional needs. The main focus for action is the teaching and learning in classrooms, in order that all students develop 'the intellectual and imaginative powers and competencies' that they need in as personalized a way as possible. Such classroom practice can only be sustained through on-going staff development. These principles characterize an approach to teacher and school development that builds on the methods and philosophy of classroom research. In Chapters 10, 11 and 12, we see how this can fit into an overall strategy for school improvement.

In the chapters that follow, these criteria will be dealt with in more detail. In the next chapter, the ways of developing a focus for classroom research projects are discussed.

FURTHER READING

One of the earliest examples of teacher-based research was the Humanities Curriculum Project and the approach is still worth considering (Stenhouse 1970, 1983). Of similar interest are the accounts of the Ford Teaching Project (Elliott and Adelman 1976) and the materials from Deakin University, for example their *Action Research Reader* (1998). There are a number of well-known articles on Lewinian action research which, although rather technical and specialized, may be of interest (see Corey 1953; Lewin 1946; Rapoport 1970; Sandford 1970). The literature on action research and critical theory is growing. Carr and Kemmis's (1986) *Becoming Critical* provides an extensive rationale for action research; Rex Gibson's (1986) *Critical Theory and Education* provides an excellent introduction, while Young's (1989) *A Critical Theory of Education* is more theoretical. A discussion of how critical theory underpins school improvement is found in *School Improvement For Real* (Chapter 2, Hopkins 2001). Of much interest is the work of Stephen Kemmis. His articles on action research (Kemmis 1983, 1988) provide an excellent overview of the topic, and the revised *Action Research Planner* (Kemmis and McTaggart 1988) not only contains a step-by-step guide, but also has useful introductory essays on action research. Background reading on the teacher-researcher movement and its educational context is found in Stenhouse's (1975) *An Introduction to Curriculum Research and Development* and in John Elliott's (1991) *Action Research for Educational Change*.

CHAPTER 5

Developing a focus

Engaging in classroom research is often initially an unnerving and occasionally threatening experience. Trying anything new involves uncertainty, and this is particularly true of teacher research. Increasingly, however, teachers are regarding the 'researching of practice' as part of their professional responsibilities. It is important therefore that the fourth criterion mentioned in the previous chapter – that of identifying and being committed to a topic for classroom research which is stated in workable terms – is adhered to. But even when this is the case, it is often difficult to establish a precise focus for the enquiry. For these reasons, in this chapter I review some ways in which teachers can develop a focus for classroom research, establish research questions and engage in theorizing. In short, this chapter deals with how to get started on classroom research.

DEVELOPING A FOCUS

Teacher research does not necessarily start with the setting of precise hypotheses! As Kemmis and McTaggart (1981: 18) point out in their first edition of *The Action Research Planner*:

> You do not have to begin with a 'problem'. All you need is a general idea that something might be improved. Your general idea may stem from a promising new idea or the recognition that existing practice falls short of aspiration. In either case you must centre attention on:
>
> - What is happening now?
> - In what sense is this problematic?
> - What can I do about it?

General starting points will look like

- I would like to improve the . . .
- Some people are unhappy about . . .
- What can I do to change the situation?
- I am perplexed by . . .
- . . . is a source of irritation. What can I do about it?
- I have an idea I would like to try out in my class.
- How can the experience of . . . be applied to . . . ?
- Just what do I do with respect to . . . ?

As you read the extract, no doubt certain ideas or topics for classroom research come to mind. These ideas may also relate to the priorities on the school's development plan, or to the school's aims, targets or mission statement. More likely they will relate to practical and immediate concerns, such as a particular aspect of a scheme of work, or a troublesome individual or class. It is worth taking a few minutes to jot down these ideas; don't worry about how well they are formed, at this stage it is more important to generate a list of topics from which one can work. Having produced a list, the next step is to evaluate the usefulness, viability and/or importance of the individual issue. There are a number of guidelines that can be of use here.

First, do not tackle issues that you cannot do anything about. For example, it may be impossible in the short or medium term to alter the banding or streaming system in your school or to change the textbook that you are using. Because you cannot do anything about it, either avoid the issue or rephrase it in a more solvable form. So, although you cannot change the textbook, it may be possible to experiment with different ways the text could be used as evidence in your classes.

Second, only take on, at least initially, small-scale and relatively limited issues. There are several reasons for this. It is important to build on success, and a small-scale project satisfactorily completed in a short space of time is reinforcing and encouraging. It is also very easy to underestimate the scale and amount of time a project will take. It is very discouraging to have found after the initial flush of enthusiasm that you have bitten off more than you can chew.

Third, choose an issue that is important to you or to your students, or one that you have to be involved with anyway in the course of your normal school activities. The topic that you focus on needs to be intrinsically motivating. If not, then again after the initial flush of enthusiasm and when the difficulties begin to build up, you will find that motivation will begin to evaporate.

Fourth, as far as possible try and work collaboratively on the focus of your classroom research. Professional partnerships, as is seen in the examples throughout the book, are a powerful form of staff development and personal support. It is also a way of reducing the isolation that some teachers work in.

Finally, make connections between your classroom research work, teaching and learning, and the school's development plan priorities or the school's aims. Although there need not be a direct relationship, it is important to relate one's individual professional enquiry to whole school initiatives and the direction in which the school is moving.

In summary, it is necessary to select an initial focus for classroom research that is viable, discrete, intrinsically interesting, involves collaboration and is related in some way to teaching and learning and whole school concerns.

PERFORMANCE GAP

A growing body of research suggests: (1) there is often incongruence between a teacher's publicly declared philosophy or beliefs about education and how he or she behaves in the classroom; (2) there is often incongruence between the teacher's declared goals and objectives and the way in which the lesson is actually taught; and (3) there is often a discrepancy between a teacher's perceptions or account of a lesson, and the perceptions or account of other participants (e.g. pupils or observers) in the classroom (see Elbaz 1983). All of these discrepancies reflect a gap between behaviour and intention. The Ford Teaching Project also monitored the 'performance gap' between teachers' aspirations and their practice. These issues have more recently been commented on in contemporary reports on the state of primary education. The 'performance gap' therefore forms an important starting point for classroom research enquiries.

Dave Ebbutt (1985) writes about 'the performance gap' as follows:

> It is via the notion of a performance gap – a gap between espoused theory and theory in action – by which advocates of action research locate its niche as an appropriate mode of research in schools and classrooms. For instance Kemmis in his *Planner* uses this illustrative example:
>
>> There is a gap between the idea and the reality of inquiry teaching in my own classroom. Recognising this gap, I must develop a strategy of action if improvements in this kind of questioning are to be achieved . . .

If you now return to the list of possible classroom research topics that you have just generated, there is probably implicit in each of the topics a description of what is currently happening (that provides a basis for reflection) and an indication of some new action connected to the existing behaviour that will lead to improvement. So, for example, in the case studies in Chapter 2, the teachers identified an existing teaching behaviour and at the same time thought of ways in which this aspect of their teaching could be improved. It is this gap between what is and what could be that is an important source of motivation in classroom research by teachers.

Ebbutt (1985) also illustrates the notion of the performance gap by posing six simple questions to demonstrate the gap between the curriculum in action and the curriculum as intention:

1 What did the pupils actually do?
2 What were they learning?
3 How worthwhile was it?
4 What did I do?
5 What did I learn?
6 What do I intend to do now?

The concept of the performance gap is useful in refining your list of topics for classroom research. The identification of a gap between what is and what could be provides motivation for change and indicates a direction for improvement. Action leads out of existing behaviours towards a new articulated goal.

OPEN AND CLOSED QUESTIONS

Implicit in much of what I have written so far is the idea that a research focus emerges out of a teacher's critical reflection on classroom experience, which is then explored through the use of the classroom research procedures. In other words, both the formation and resolution of the research enquiry is grounded in the teacher's experience.

The formation of a research focus or question occurs within either an open or closed context. Open questions take as their starting point a teacher's critical reflection on his or her teaching. This reflection culminates in a decision to utilize classroom research techniques to understand more fully and then develop his or her teaching (using the techniques discussed in the following four chapters). Sandra, in the first example in Chapter 2, started from an open position and developed hypotheses about her teaching by using classroom research procedures. Having identified a focus, Sandra then developed a plan for action. Similarly, the teachers working collaboratively in the third example in Chapter 2 also started from an open position. The open approach, then, is one where teachers engage in classroom research as a reflective activity. From this reflection they derive questions that can be researched and that subsequently provide a basis for action.

The closed approach deviates from the open insofar as many teachers have already identified a specific issue or hypothesis before engaging in classroom research. In this instance, their classroom research begins with the testing of a hypothesis or exploring a specific activity. So with the example of Ann in Chapter 2, who, having heard about a new teaching method that applied to her subject area, used classroom research to invest-igate the effectiveness of the approach. In this case, the focus on teaching strategies had immediate and direct relevance for classroom practice.

Later in this chapter, there is a more extensive discussion of formu-lating evaluation questions. Although the purpose there is specifically evalu-ation, rather than classroom research more generally, the same principles apply. The *open* approach is characterized as:

- take a broad area of enquiry
- carry out the initial enquiry
- gradually focus the enquiry.

By way of contrast, the *closed* approach typically follows this sequence:

- take a specific issue
- derive research questions
- choose an appropriate methodology.

The difference between open and closed reflects the derivation of the focus. In the first instance, the hypothesis or question emerges as a result of critical reflection; in the second, it is a given, and the teacher having refined it proceeds to the enquiry. Both approaches reflect classroom research as it is defined in this book, because in both instances the research is controlled by the teacher for the purpose of improving practice. The contrast between open and closed questions or hypotheses can also be represented in diagrammatic form as in Figure 5.1.

Type	Hypothesis
Open	Generating
Closed	Testing

Figure 5.1

Dillon (1983) has produced a similar (if rather more academic) schema for conceptualizing 'problem formation'. He writes:

> Three existential levels of problem and three corresponding psy-chological activities can be identified as forming part of those events which may be appropriately designated as problem finding. In ex-istential terms, a problem can be existent, emergent or potential.

Problem level (existential/ psychological)	Problem ———————	Activity———————	Solution
1 existing/evident	. . . as problematic	Perceiving the situation (Recognition)	. . . as resolved
2 emergent/implicit	. . . for elements of a problem	Probing the data (Discovery)	. . . for elements of a solution
3 potential/inchoate	. . . a defined problem	Producing the problem-event (Invention)	. . . a defined solution

Figure 5.2 A conceptual scheme for comparing levels of problem finding and solving.

An existent problem has fully-developed being and appearance in the phenomenological field of events facing the observer. In psychological terms, the problem is evident and the observer perceives, recognizes, and identifies it. At a second, less developed level an emergent problem exists which is implicit rather than evident. After probing the data – nosing about in the field of events, so to speak – the observer discovers or 'finds it'. At a still less developed level, a potential problem exists. No problem in an onto-logical sense exists *qua* problem, but constituent elements are present, striking the observer as an inchoate problem. By combin-ing these and other elements in some way, the observer creates, produces or invents a problem. These descriptive terms relate the existential and psychological dimensions of problem finding activ-ity at three levels, as follows [see Figure 5.2].

My purpose of going into such detail about developing research questions, or what others call 'problem formation', is simply to legitimize the position of teachers who want to engage in classroom research just to find out about their teaching. Classroom research is not solely about ex-ploring specific 'problems' or testing explicit hypotheses. It is appropriate for teachers to use classroom research as a means of critically reflecting on their teaching and developing hypotheses about it.

FORMULATING HYPOTHESES

Whether or not teachers are initially involved in open or closed problems, they will have to formulate hypotheses or questions at some stage. As I suggested in Chapter 4, the teacher-researcher, either as an individual or as a member of a group, needs to define his or her problem clearly, for it is this definition that determines what data are collected and analysed. It is inevitable that our observations tend to be theory-laden, so consequently it is important to formulate as explicitly as one can the hypotheses that are being tested or the research questions one wishes to explore. If, for example, a group of teachers are concerned about the problem of initiating classroom discussion, they may first hypothesize that asking more open-ended questions would encourage freer responses; a number of different hypotheses could be developed and tested around this contingency. The hypotheses, however, need to be extremely clear and precise. Because there are so many variables in the complex art of teaching, even a carefully worded hypothesis can sometimes only be reported as tentative and provisional. Pring (1978) gives some examples of classroom research hypotheses taken from the Ford Teaching project:

> In order to cut out 'the guessing game' and move from a formal to an informal pattern, teachers may have to refrain from the following acts:
>
> 1 Changing topic
> Hypothesis. When teachers change the topic under discussion, they may prevent pupils from expressing and developing their own ideas, since pupils tend to interpret such interventions as attempts to get conformity to a particular line of reasoning.
>
> 2 Positive reinforcers
> Hypothesis. Utterances like 'good', 'interesting', 'right', in response to ideas expressed can prevent the expression and discussion of alternative ideas, since pupils tend to interpret them as attempts to legitimate the development of some ideas rather than others.

Following Popper's answer to the problem of induction (see Magee 1973: Ch. 2), it is more appropriate to formulate hypotheses as unambiguously as we can, so as to expose them as clearly as possible to refutation. For as Popper pointed out, although empirical generalizations are in principle not verifiable, they are falsifiable and, consequently, they can be tested by systematic attempts to refute them.

THE CASE OF CURRICULUM EVALUATION

Many of the issues related to 'Developing a Focus' for classroom research have been paralleled in recent years by developments in curriculum evaluation. Although many curriculum evaluations were initially 'externally funded', increasingly much of this evaluation activity became school-based. Unfortunately, this approach to evaluation, instead of building on the traditions of classroom research, has remained wedded to an academic view of evaluation that is based on the ubiquitous evaluation report. Yet evaluations that have an improvement perspective, provide a structure for teachers and others to subject a particular curriculum change to their own professional judgement and, in so doing, to improve the programme and make further plans for implementation. In this way, an evaluation can, like classroom research, provide a means for translating an educational idea into practice as well as monitoring and enhancing curriculum development. This was the central theme of my book *Evaluation for School Development* (Hopkins 1989), where I tried to outline an approach to evaluation that was:

- built on the best practice of classroom research insofar as it supported development and was linked to classroom practice;
- sufficiently pragmatic to serve the decision-making purposes of evaluation; and
- as far as possible fitted into the day-to-day life of the school.

The reason for discussing curriculum evaluation at this point is twofold. The first is that one of the approaches to school-focused evaluation described in the book was based around the use of the evaluation or research question that is one of the themes of this chapter. The second is that the structure of curriculum evaluation provides another model or format for conducting whole school, teacher research. In the following example, I describe two approaches to the formulation of questions in an evaluation we did of 'Technology Across the Curriculum' (TAC) (see Figure 5.3).

An evaluation question is, simply, a question that can be answered by some form of structured investigation or research. In this context, it is important to:

- Avoid grandiose questions outside the scope of formative evaluation, such as: 'Is TAC a "Good Thing"?'
- Avoid long-term questions outside the time frame: 'Are this year's students getting a better experience of Technology?'
- Avoid questions that are only answerable by large-scale or very technical research.
- Aim for suitably defined questions that can be addressed through the limited quantity of data you can be expected to collect.

Although the formulation of questions is often quite challenging, this should not deter us from confronting tough 'bottom line' issues that reflect the various stages in the change process. Obviously, not all the following questions will apply to every evaluation, but the following examples are the

1 *A linear approach*

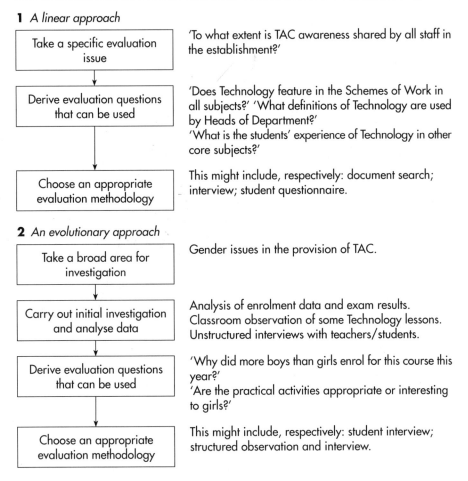

Take a specific evaluation issue

'To what extent is TAC awareness shared by all staff in the establishment?'

Derive evaluation questions that can be used

'Does Technology feature in the Schemes of Work in all subjects?' 'What definitions of Technology are used by Heads of Department?'
'What is the students' experience of Technology in other core subjects?'

Choose an appropriate evaluation methodology

This might include, respectively: document search; interview; student questionnaire.

2 *An evolutionary approach*

Take a broad area for investigation

Gender issues in the provision of TAC.

Carry out initial investigation and analyse data

Analysis of enrolment data and exam results. Classroom observation of some Technology lessons. Unstructured interviews with teachers/students.

Derive evaluation questions that can be used

'Why did more boys than girls enrol for this course this year?'
'Are the practical activities appropriate or interesting to girls?'

Choose an appropriate evaluation methodology

This might include, respectively: student interview; structured observation and interview.

Figure 5.3 Formulating evaluation questions.

types of questions that will help us assess the impact of a curriculum change on student achievement and the process of school improvement:

- What changes have occurred in teachers' or students' knowledge base?
- What changes have occurred in teachers' or students' skill level and use?
- What changes have occurred in teachers' or students' opinions and feelings?
- What changes have occurred in the culture or organization of the school?
- What changes have occurred in student tests or examinations?

This general approach to evaluation includes four major activities:

1 *Agree on evaluation questions.* Generating questions helps focus the evaluation. Often the questions will relate to the school development plan

Question	Source	Collection method	Responsibility	Time-line
How was the plan for the delivery of TAC formulated? Was the process effective?	TAC co-ordinator; school co-ordinator	Interviews	Evaluator	Oct.–Dec.
What is the plan? Why was this method of delivery chosen?	TAC/school co-ordinators; staff	Review documents; question-naires; interviews	TAC co-ordinator; evaluator	Jan.–Mar.
Have students received 10% balanced TAC? Does the reality reflect the plan?	Staff; students	Interviews; question-naires	Co-ordinator; evaluator	Easter onward

Figure 5.4 A practical evaluation schedule.

priorities. It is important not to be too ambitious about the number and scope of the questions asked.

2 *Determine information needs and collection methods.* Once the questions are generated, clarified and prioritized, some way of answering them has to be devised. Potential information sources and collection methods should be identified for each evaluation question. The more sources and methods used, the greater the likelihood that the information will be valid. One way of structuring this important stage in the design of the evaluation is to use a simple worksheet as outlined in Figure 5.4. As you begin to formulate your evaluation question(s) and devise appropriate data-gathering methods, it is helpful to 'cost' them in terms of (1) the time it will take to complete the work and (2) the time and people available to you. The plan shown in Figure 5.4 is an example of an evaluation schedule for Technology Across the Curriculum (TAC).

3 *Collect and analyse information.* This activity should co-exist with data collection. Early checks allow evaluators to seek new information sources if necessary and to identify emerging and unanticipated outcomes.

4 *Reports.* Feedback should normally occur as soon as possible, be tailored to its audience and include follow-up activities if required. This may include reporting to governors and parents and providing information for the school's next development plan. The reports need not be written; they may be given orally with handouts containing summaries of data as

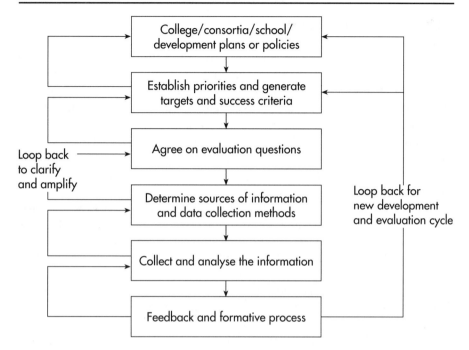

Figure 5.5 The evaluation process.

'back-up' material. Often, reduced data are sufficient to act as a basis for discussion. When reports are written they should be short; usually data summaries can be prepared on one side of A4. They should also distinguish clearly between the presentation of data and any interpretation that may be made of the results.

An overview of this evaluation process is given in Figure 5.5. This figure is of course far more linear than the action research cycle described in the previous chapter, in reality, a number of these steps co-exist and time-lines tend to merge. It may also be that questions have to be refined and unanticipated logistical problems may occur during the evaluation. An obvious precaution is to ensure that time-lines are realistic, that one is not expecting too much too soon, and that as many problems as possible are anticipated.

Two further points need to be made about this process. The first is that there needs to be a logic or flow between the evaluation question, the data collected, analysis, feedback and the resulting action. In that way, the evaluation develops a power of its own because each stage builds on the other. The second is to make certain that the evaluation questions are important to the school and staff concerned. Evaluation is so time-consuming that its results should not be gratuitous, but feed real need and be able to provide useful and pertinent information.

THEORY AND THEORIZING

Finally a word about theory. So far, I have used the word in two distinct senses. The first refers to a set of personal assumptions, beliefs or presuppositions that individuals hold. Our view of the world, our individual construction of reality is at one level essentially theoretical. The second use of the word is in the more traditional or 'grand' sense, where theory refers to a coherent set of assumptions which purport to explain, predict and be used as a guide to practice. This is the sense in which the word was used when Ann, in the case study in Chapter 2, turned to theory in order to inform her classroom research problem.

Unfortunately, all too often educational theory in this second sense is not all that useful in telling us in a practical way how to behave in the classroom. In many instances, the gap between theory and practice is so large that it prevents any useful connection. This occurs because our theories are often not specific enough, or the propositions they contain are not easily generalized to individual situations. This, of course, is an unsatisfactory situation, and one that argues for a different approach to educational theory.

A viable alternative is to theorize about practice, and theorizing is a third way in which we can understand theory. Theorizing approaches theory through practice (the reverse of grand theory, which goes from theory to practice), much in the same way as the hypotheses, assumptions and constructs we develop from classroom research procedures emerge from data gathered from actual classroom experiences. The discussion of grounded theory in Chapter 9 illustrates how theory can be generated from data gathered in a substantive situation. When we are engaged in classroom research, we can be said to be engaged in educational theorizing because we are reflecting systematically and critically on practice. As Richard Pring (1978: 244–5) writes:

> Such systematic and critical examination will involve philosophizing, appealing to evidence, reference to . . . theories. But there is no reason for saying that it will add up to a theory. [Classroom research is about] helping the practitioner to theorize, i.e. think more systematically, critically and intelligently about his or her practice.

You will remember that Stenhouse (1975) in his discussion of the teacher-researcher illustrates this attitude when he suggested that the teacher, instead of accepting uncritically what a particular theory claims, implements it in the form of a working hypothesis or curriculum proposal. This thought captures two of the fundamental aspects of what Donald Schön (1991) has called the 'reflective practitioner'. In educational terms, such professional teachers (a) stand in control of knowledge rather than being subservient to it and (b) by doing this they are engaged in the process of theorizing and achieving self-knowledge.

The idea of 'self-knowledge' is an important one in this context. It refers to the individual internalization of ideas that empowers the person. It refers to those moments of clarity and power that occur when we understand a concept and see how we can use it in our personal or professional lives. It is an exciting and exhilarating moment and one which, for teachers and pupils alike, is too rare in our schools. This, as I understand it, is the basis of Polanyi's (1973) writing on *Personal Knowledge*. Personal knowledge is that which is mediated through subjective experience and subsequently owned by the individual. The most pertinent feature of Polanyi's work is the concept of tacit knowledge, the knowledge we cannot articulate. He suggests that we know a great deal more than we can put into words, and that we sense and understand more than we can describe or explain. An aspiration of the approach to classroom research adopted in this book is for teachers to gain more clarity on their 'tacit knowledge' and to incorporate this in their teaching.

Walt Whitman (1855/1959) captures a similar thought in this evocative passage from *Leaves of Grass*:

> You shall no longer take things at second or third hand . . . nor look through the eyes of the dead . . . nor feed on the spectres in books,
> You shall not look through my eyes either, nor take things from me,
> You shall listen to all sides and filter them from yourself.

In this chapter, I have discussed the challenges involved in developing a focus for classroom research by teachers. I have been at pains to point out that the focus of an enquiry can be either open or closed insofar as the teacher is engaged in hypothesis generation or testing. I have also pointed to some ways in which the focus of classroom research can be clarified and made more specific, and linked the whole discussion to a notion of theorizing and self-knowledge. The underlying theme is that through developing a focus for their research, teachers gain more control over their professional lives.

The advice in this chapter obviously applies to both teachers working alone or in collaboration. For reasons already rehearsed in previous chapters, I believe that collaborative efforts at teacher research are to be preferred. Talking to others, for example, is an excellent way of clarifying the focus of a research enquiry. In the next three chapters, we discuss practical ways in which data about the focus of a classroom research enquiry can be gathered.

FURTHER READING

The third edition of *The Action Research Planner* by Stephen Kemmis and Robin McTaggart (1988) contains detailed and helpful advice on 'finding a theme' for classroom research. Other helpful sources for 'getting started' are Judith Bell's (1999) *Doing Your Research Project* and Jean McNiff's (1992) *Action Research: Principles and Practice*. More specific foci for classroom research enquiries are comprehensively illustrated in Good and Brophy's (1997) *Looking in Classrooms*. A description of evaluation techniques and approaches similar in aspiration and application to the strategies described in this book is found in *Evaluation for School Development* (Hopkins 1989). For a discussion of hypothesis generation, it is useful to look at some of the Ford Teaching Project materials (see Elliott 1976). The article by Dillon (1983) on problem finding is very informative. Bryan Magee's (1973) monograph on Popper is a paragon of clarity and neatly summarizes Popper's solution to the problem of induction. Donald Schön's (1991) *The Reflective Practitioner*, although not specifically about education, echoes many of the themes of this book, particularly in regard to how professionals develop and learn through reflection and action.

CHAPTER 6

Principles of classroom observation

Observation plays a crucial role not only in classroom research, but also more generally in supporting the professional growth of teachers and in the process of school development. In my experience, it seems to be the pivotal activity that links together reflection for the individual teacher and collaborative enquiry for pairs or groups of teachers. It also encourages the development of a language for talking about teaching and provides a means for working on developmental priorities for the staff as a whole. This chapter is therefore of central importance. I begin by outlining five criteria crucial to the successful practice of classroom observation, then describe the generic three-stage cycle of classroom observation and its specific application to partnership teaching and conclude by making some suggestions for training activities. In discussing the principles underlying observation, the emphasis is not just on classroom research, but also more generally on teacher and school development. The following chapter is devoted to a description of four methods of undertaking classroom observation: *open*, *focused*, *structured* and *systematic* observation.

KEY FEATURES OF CLASSROOM OBSERVATION

Although I believe that, in general, classroom observation is a 'good thing', there are a number of specific skills associated with it which, if not acquired, can have disastrous results for the morale of individuals and the whole staff. The main problem, it seems to me, is that often we jump too quickly to conclusions about the behaviour of others. As I note in Chapter 9, the philosopher Karl Popper claims that, 'observations . . . are [always] interpretations in the light of theories' (Magee 1973: 107). Although we constantly need to use our personal theories to construct our worlds (and without doing so would not survive long in the classroom!), this uniquely human intuition is not the greatest asset during classroom observation. Moving to judgement too quickly is one of the main characteristics of poor observation. There are at least five key features of classroom observation that need to characterize our approach if the process is to lead to professional growth.

Joint planning

A joint planning meeting is of crucial importance, especially if it precedes the first in a series of observations. There is a need to establish at the outset a climate of trust between observer and observed, to agree on a focus that both regard as worthwhile, to discuss the context of the lesson, to sort out the 'ground rules' – time and place of the observation, where to sit, how to interact with the pupils, how long to spend in the classroom, etc. The more specific and focused the observation, the more there is a need for joint planning. Once the observer and the observed become familiar with each other's style and the roles are reversed, then the time spent in the initial meeting can be reduced. It may also be possible during an on-going cycle of observations to combine feedback and planning meetings.

Focus

There are two broad ways of categorizing the focus of classroom observation activities: general or specific. The terms are self-explanatory: the former indicating an approach where 'everything counts' and therefore could be commented on; and the latter where the observation is confined to a particular or well-defined classroom activity or teaching practice. When the focus is broad, the more likely it is that the observer, who having no criteria to turn to, will rely on 'subjective' judgements to interpret what is going on in the classroom. Although these judgements may be perfectly valid, they most probably will be of little use to the teacher being observed unless the basis for them has been discussed and agreed on in advance. The danger in this situation is that the teacher being observed is subject to a series of 'mini-judgements' on his or her teaching that tell you more about the educational values of the observer than the teacher whose classroom practice is under scrutiny. The more specific and negotiated the focus of the classroom observation, the more likely it is that the 'data' so gathered will be useful for developmental purposes. If the focus for classroom observation relates to the development plan, then the observation could contribute both to teacher and school development.

Establishing criteria

The contribution of classroom observation to professional development is greatly enhanced if, during the initial discussion, criteria for the observation are established. I remember vividly during an interview on our evaluation of the 'School Teacher Appraisal' project, asking an appraiser, the head of a primary school, what criteria she used when observing her colleagues. 'We don't use checklists in this school', she replied angrily. 'Come on', I said, 'What were you looking for when you went into the classroom?' 'Oh', she said, 'Were the children smiling and engaged in their work? Was the classroom environment attractive? Was the work they were doing appropriate for their ability?', and so on. Before too long she had given me a fairly sophisticated description of 'good primary practice'. What a pity I thought that the staff of that primary school had not had that discussion before the start of the appraisal process. Criteria are nothing to be frightened of, particularly if they are negotiated and agreed *before* the start of an observation. It may be helpful for the staff as a whole to agree and develop criteria on a particular classroom observation before the cycle of observation begins. It is also important that such criteria are subject to on-going review as those involved refine their definitions of good practice. When viewed in this way, the discussion of criteria can act as a 'road map' for development as well as providing standards by which to discuss the outcomes of an observation.

Observation skills

There are three main 'skills' involved here. The first is guarding against the natural tendency to move too quickly into judgement. This can be achieved to some extent, as we have seen already, by having a clear focus for the observation and agreeing the ground rules beforehand. Second, there are the interpersonal skills involved when 'invading another person's space'; this includes creating a sense of trust and being supportive in situations where the other person may feel threatened. The third skill area is more technical. It is knowing how to design schedules that will allow the observer to gather appropriate information on classroom behaviour or transactions, or of knowing which are the most appropriate checklists or *aide-mémoires* to use in a particular situation. This latter point is especially important, as one obviously wishes to avoid having the values underlying an observation schedule imposing themselves on the outcomes of the feedback discussion.

Feedback

The benefits of classroom observation will only be realized if appropriate feedback is given. Put another way, poor feedback is characterized by being rushed, judgemental, one-way and impressionistic. As has already been implied, feedback appears to work best if:

- it is given within 24 hours of the observation,
- it is based on careful and systematic recording,
- it is based on factual data,
- the factual data are interpreted with reference to known and agreed criteria,
- the interpretation comes in the first instance from the teacher who has been observed,
- it is given as part of a two-way discussion, and
- it leads to the development of strategies for building on what has been learnt.

THE THREE-PHASE OBSERVATION CYCLE

These key features lay the basis for a professional development approach to classroom observation. The 'three-phase observation cycle', originally called 'clinical supervision', was initially developed in North America as a method of supervising student teachers, but it is well suited for use in classroom research situations.

   The three essential phases of this classroom observation process are a planning meeting, the classroom observation itself and a feedback discussion. The *planning meeting* provides the observer and teacher with an opportunity to reflect on the proposed lesson, and this leads to a mutual decision to collect observational data on an aspect of the teacher's classroom practice. During the *classroom observation* phase, the observer observes the teacher in the classroom and collects objective data on that aspect of the teaching or learning they agreed upon earlier. It is during the *feedback discussion* that the observer and teacher share the information gathered during the observation, decide on appropriate action, agree a record of the discussion, and often plan another round of observation. An outline of the process is given in Figure 6.1. It is important to realize that to be effective, all three phases of the process need to be gone through systematically.

   There are a number of principles that are important to consider in this approach to classroom observation. First, the climate of interaction between teacher and observer needs to be non-threatening, helping and one of mutual trust. Second, the focus of the activity should be on improving classroom practice and the reinforcing of successful strategies, rather than on criticism of unsuccessful patterns of behaviour, or changing the teacher's personality. Third, the process depends on the collection and use of objective observational data, not unsubstantiated value judgements. Fourth, teachers are encouraged to make inferences about their teaching from the data, and to use the data to construct 'hypotheses' that can be tested out in the future. Next, each cycle of observation is part of an on-going process that builds on the other. Finally, both observer and teacher

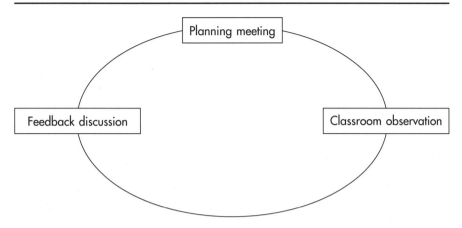

Figure 6.1 The three-phase observation cycle.

are engaged in a mutual process of professional development that can lead to improvement in teaching and observational skills for both. In all these ways, classroom observation can support both specific purposes, as well as the more general aspirations of teacher and school development.

An example of the three-phase approach to classroom observation is given by Marsha and George.

Marsha had already observed several of George's year 8 History classes. During a planning conference, they went over George's lesson plan. George identified his objectives, one of which was to involve as many pupils as possible in discussing a particular historical event. They decided to focus the observation on the type of questions George asked and the pupils' responses. Marsha suggested she use a seating plan on which to 'tally' the voluntary and solicited comments from the pupils. George agreed and also requested that she jot down his questions verbatim.

During the lesson, Marsha recorded information for the 20 minutes George had planned for the discussion. Afterwards, as they went over the data, patterns began to emerge. George noticed that, although the discussion had been lively, only 12 out of the 28 pupils had participated (he had thought during the lesson that more were involved). Also, certain types of questions tended to elicit more complete responses.

They both decided that it might be useful if George sequenced his questions from factual types (to establish a common knowledge base) to more open-ended, opinion questions. Also, now that he knew which pupils were reticent, George would attempt to involve them more in class discussions. Marsha suggested a couple of techniques that worked for her, and George was excited about trying them out. The feedback conference ended with both agreeing to use the same observation focus in the near future to compare the results of George's new strategies.

PARTNERSHIP OBSERVATION

The three-phase cycle provides a general framework for classroom observation which is particularly relevant to 'partnership' teaching or collaborative observation. I try to encourage teachers to engage in classroom research in pairs or small groups for a number of reasons. Among them is the emotional support they gain from each other, particularly as this activity is initially threatening. It is now fairly well established that teachers learn best from other teachers, and take criticism most easily from this source. It is ideal if teachers in cross-hierarchical groups can act as observers for each other, and this mutual exchange of roles quickly breaks down barriers which otherwise may be monolithic.

The observer in the partnership can play any number of differing roles. He or she can observe a lesson in general, focus on specific aspects of the teaching and talk to pupils all during one observation period. This lightens the teacher's problem of analysis and tends to increase the objectivity of the data gathered. In addition, the observer may also be able to note incidents that the teacher would ordinarily miss.

Colleagues involved in the University of Cambridge Institute of Education and Bedfordshire Education Service 'Developing Successful Learning Project' refined an approach to classroom observation that emphasizes the partnership role. The following description is taken from their work.

This approach to partnership observation assumes that:

- all teachers can develop their practice, and
- all students can learn successfully.

It is based on the following principles:

- practice can only be improved in the contexts in which it normally occurs, and
- individuals need the support of colleagues as they seek to develop their practice.

The central strategy is to create partnerships of teachers who are committed to helping one another develop their classroom practice. These partnerships usually involve two or three colleagues who, for the purposes of this work, regard one another as equals. A partner must be somebody with whom you can work comfortably.

Before the observation, a number of issues have to be considered and decisions made by the partners:

- the role of the observer in the classroom,
- the confidentiality of discussions,
- commitment to the programme,
- date/time place of observation,
- date/time place of *review* – this should be set as near to the observation as possible (within 24 hours); the place must be one without interruptions, on or off site, and needs to be non-threatening; it is best to allow a minimum of 40 minutes for the review,
- how often observation is to take place – this is dependent on the time-table and the availability of cover,
- which classes and lessons are to be observed,
- whether this is to be a focused or unfocused observation, and
- methods of observation to be used.

During the observation, the observer should only record what is seen or heard and not be judgemental or intrusive. Time should also be found for one or two minutes of positive discussion at the end of the observation period. This will allow the observed teacher to release any tension that may have developed during the lesson. The observer may also give the class teacher a copy of the observation notes.

During the review discussion, feedback should be non-threatening, supportive and based on the information gathered during the observation. *Target setting* evolves from feedback, and once this has been given it is time to identify one area of learning to be developed. Targets must be realistic and attainable within the designated time-span. This does not, however, preclude the developments continuing over an extended period. If successful, these changes often become an integral part of effective class teaching, thus enhancing the learning experience of students.

Action planning for development is based on the answers to a series of questions that need to be addressed before modifying teaching practice:

- What do I want to achieve?
- How am I going to achieve this?
- How will this improve the quality of learning?
- How will this development be evaluated?
- Will I involve the pupils in the process of monitoring and evaluation?
- Are there adequate resources to implement the proposed development?

If, after carrying out the *action plan*, the outcomes were not successful, do not be discouraged! Try to discover why. This is where assistance and advice from a 'third person' could be invaluable. Perhaps you were too ambitious in your objectives; if so, return to target setting. If the objective was realistic, it may have been the way in which it was developed in the class; if this was the case, return to the *action plan*. If the outcomes were successful, why were they? Always reflect on practice. The partnership may now wish to continue with the original target, or a new target may be set.

Examples from the work of the 'Developing Successful Learning Project' have already been given in Chapter 2. This further example of partnership observation, prepared by Pamela Hughes of Sharnbrook Upper School, focuses on involving students in the observation process.

This classroom project placed particular emphasis on the idea of student involvement. There are 29 students in the class. The project included the following steps:

1 Initially the students in the two classes involved were given letters to take home, to explain their involvement and to give parents an opportunity to contact us if they wished.
2 The students, working in groups, discussed and then listed things which (a) helped their learning and (b) hindered their learning within the class. (This took 10 minutes in one class and 30 in the other where it was used as an oral exercise.)
3 After the observation, the students in my class were very keen to be involved further. They knew that the focus would be evaluating group work, but they did not know the specific areas.

We discussed ways of evaluating our learning, but not in those terms! The outcomes, from the students, were recorded by further observation, videotaping and by questionnaire (testing was not mentioned). I explained that I had already designed a questionnaire. Somebody asked if the class could compile their own – we debated time, costs, what it would include, how to go about it, etc.

I decided to let them try during the following lesson. I was able to do this because they were year 9 and the task was suitable for an English lesson. I think this would have been more difficult to organize in other areas of the curriculum. They were also keen to video the lesson and one student was made responsible for setting it up in the corner of the room before the beginning of the lesson.

I began to think of my *action plan* when they undertook the task, i.e. using the board for key points and ensuring a better mix within groups.

The lesson

The video: It was difficult to decide where to focus as we did not want it to be intrusive. The students decided that they would focus the camera on one side of the room and that half-way through a designated person would change its direction. The lesson followed afternoon registration and so there was no difficulty in setting the camera up prior to the class arriving.

The observation: This was unscheduled. We were just about to begin the lesson when a member of the class asked if one of them could observe as the other teacher had. I 'thought on my feet' and could not see any objection. I asked for a volunteer and chose the first hand that shot up. I knew that I did not have time to explain about how to do observation, so placed him in a position from where he could see most of the class and told him to write down anything that he thought might be affecting our learning. This would by nature be judgemental and for 'my eyes only'.

The task: The aim was for each group to produce a questionnaire which would be used by a group, not an individual. Whole class discussion (using the board for key points), followed by paired friendship groups. Further brainstorming as a class, followed by each pair joining another. I chose the groupings.

Follow-up

I used the student observation notes and the video with my teaching partner, Christine. We were both surprised at the candid nature of the observation notes. Groups of students have also seen extracts from the video (during lunch-times) and this has led to further discussion. One 'spin-off' from the student involvement has been greater tolerance of individuals within the class and the building of a more positive class identity.

Notes made by the class member
(The comments in brackets have been added by Pamela Hughes.)

Beginning of lesson: everybody is chatting quietly. Then group task is
   explained. Groups are scattered around the room. (Group task in
   pairs.)
Same groups (pairs) as they are sitting in. They begin the group
   discussion. One pair messing around.

Everybody works with somebody of the same sex.

Groups talking.

People at the back of the class are working more than the people towards the front.

Another member of staff enters – pupils cease to work and then get back to what they were doing before they entered.

Class discussion: Most people are contributing to the questions.

Some people had very good questions.

Some doodling in their notebooks while class discussion.

Nobody talked between themselves during this part of class discussion.

A couple of people are chewing pencils, pens.

Some people seem to be getting bored.

Groups combine: People only joined in a mixed group when there was no other choice.

Once the groups had been rearranged there was new discussion.

People who did not want to really work together in groups are working better than groups made up of just friends.

The people working best are the people with the camera directed towards them.

Most of the groups seem to have forgotten about the camera.

People who are messing around at the beginning seem to have calmed down a bit.

When the camera was moved for a second time people who had been fairly quiet up until now suddenly started moving and talking.

The people who are not in the picture now relax and start playing the fool to the camera. (I collated the group tasks some had not finished. Those who finished quickly began designing the layout.)

Quick response from all to correct teacher. (I cannot remember what this was – it may have been homework.)

Bell goes, chattering began and people started to pack away, but Mrs Hughes stopped them straight away.

TRAINING FOR OBSERVATION

Classroom observation can be a sensitive issue for teachers unused to regular or systematic observation since their teacher training and early days in the profession. It is also associated in many teachers' minds with accountability procedures such as inspection, appraisal, evaluation and performance management. As I am arguing in this book however, observation is something that can be valuable in its own right and used for a variety of staff development and school improvement purposes. Experience suggests that initial apprehension disappears once the process of observation is under way, providing appropriate procedures are used. I have already discussed some of the main principles of classroom observation, and it may be useful in concluding this chapter to briefly describe some training activities that can be used to promote good practice.

The first activity is designed to acquaint participants with the three-phase cycle of classroom observation. The activity utilizes video examples to provide 'action images' which participants can relate to their own experience. The session could be divided into five parts:

1 Overview of benefits of the three-phase cycle.

2 Video example of the planning meeting. In discussing the video, participants may wish to consider:

   - How important is negotiation in the whole process?
   - What skills are involved?
   - What is the relationship between the participants?
   - How realistic is the agreed focus?

3 Video example of the classroom observation. During the video, participants should be encouraged to keep in mind the agreed focus of the observation and make notes on it as if they were in the classroom. In discussing the video, participants may wish to consider:

   - What other areas of focus could have been identified?
   - How feasible was it to obtain information on the agreed focus?
   - What skills are needed by the observer?
   - What are the relative benefits of open or focused observation?

4 Video example of the feedback discussion. In discussing the video, participants may wish to consider:

   - How far do you agree with the points raised in the discussion?
   - What is the balance between judgement and reflection in the discussion?
   - How far can this discussion lay the basis for professional growth?
   - What skills are required by an observer in promoting the developmental nature of such a discussion?

5 Review the classroom observation process in relation to the five key issues discussed earlier.

The second activity is designed to aid thinking about which areas to focus on in classroom observation and suitable data collection methods. Each group member should in turn select an aspect of their work as a possible focus for classroom observation and outline it to the group. The remainder of the group should then discuss:

- What information could be gathered through classroom observation?
- How would the observer collect it?
- How would the observer record it?
- What are the criteria that could most helpfully be applied to this particular aspect of the teacher's work?

As each member of the group presents an example and the others respond to it, the group should build up an *aide-mémoire* using the box below. The *aide-mémoire* may then be helpful in designing appropriate observation instruments or schedules and for identifying the most appropriate criteria to inform the feedback discussion.

Area of focus	Information needs	How to collect	How to record	Criteria

If possible, back in school, participants should ask a colleague to use the approach devised during this exercise in their classroom and then to report back to other colleagues on how well it worked. Experience suggests that 'dry runs' such as this, assist enormously in the process of acquiring the skills of, and allaying fears about, classroom observation.

As the examples in this chapter demonstrate, classroom observation can provide powerful insights into classroom practice, as well as being a means of professional development and a major tool for the classroom researcher. In the chapter, I have described some of the main principles involved in doing classroom observation as well as providing a series of examples which hopefully give a feel of the method in practice and some suggestions for training activities. I have emphasized the partnership approach to observation because I feel that it is here where the link between teacher and school development lies, especially if the focus of the observation is related to whole school issues. In the following chapter, we look more closely at the methods available to the classroom observer committed to enhancing classroom practice.

FURTHER READING

The 'clinical supervision' approach to classroom observation, on which this three-phase approach was based, is described in a practical way by Acheson and Gall (1992) in their *Techniques in the Clinical Supervision of Teachers*. The other classic texts on clinical supervision are by Goldhammer *et al.* (1980) and Cogan (1973). The work of Jean Rudduck contains a number of examples of teachers in partnership (Rudduck 1982, 1991; Rudduck and Sigsworth 1985). Colin Hook's (1981) *Studying Classrooms* contains a detailed discussion of the place of classroom observation in teacher research, and Judith Bell's (1999) helpful book on research in general contains a rationale for a more traditional approach to classroom observation.

CHAPTER 7

Methods of observation in classroom research

Within the general framework of the three-phase classroom observation or partnership teaching approach, there is no one best method to use. When teachers observe each other teach, all they often require are simple ways of gathering information on basic topics, such as questioning techniques, on- or off-task behaviour, and classroom management. It is usually preferable for teachers to devise their own observation schedules, to invent them for a specific purpose. By doing this, there is usually more ownership developed over the subject of the observation and a better fit between the focus of the observation and the data-gathering method.

Before devising the observation checklist, it is often useful to ask some organizing questions in order to clarify the purpose of the observation. These questions are illustrative:

- What is the purpose of the observation?
- What is the focus of the observation?
- What teacher/student behaviours are important to observe?
- What data-gathering methods will best serve the purpose?
- How will the data be used?

These and similar questions should help the teachers involved clarify how easy it is to use the chosen approach, how much the observer looks at and how far the observer makes judgements.

The next step is to decide on the observation method. Although there are many approaches, it is possible to categorize them into four main groups. Each of them could involve the use of 'pencil and paper', audio- or video-recording. They are open observation, focused observation, structured observation and systematic observation.

OPEN OBSERVATION

In this approach, the observer literally uses a blank sheet of paper to record the lesson. The observer either notes down key points about the lesson or uses a personal form of shorthand for making a verbatim recording of classroom transactions. For example:

> *Teacher*: Turn 2 p. 46. Mary give us y. ans. to q. 1.
> *Mary*:   WW II was partly t. result of unresolved conflicts of WW I.
> *Teacher*: That's 1 pt. of the ans. John give us y. ans.

The aim is usually to enable subsequent reconstruction of the lesson. A variation of this approach is to agree to record only those events that fit into certain broad categories or under certain headings, as shown in Figure 7.1.

The observer should aim to record factual and descriptive information.
Teaching skills

(i) Presentation	
(ii) Indirect teaching	
(iii) Direct teaching	
(iv) Voice	
(v) Questioning strategies	
(vi) Feedback	
(vii) Subject matter	
(viii) Expectations	

Figure 7.1 An example of open observation (from Bollington and Bradley 1990).

A problem with this approach is that it is often unfocused and can lead to premature judgements. The best way to handle this approach is to make open recording as factual as possible and leave interpretation until a discussion after the lesson. Because of its general nature, it is important to stick closely to each component of the three-phase cycle; otherwise what began as a mutual approach to observation could result in a one-way monologue!

> **In this extended example, Heather Lockhart describes how she went about observing her colleague Maureen's teaching.**
>
> Maureen has recently begun to doubt the effectiveness of her questioning techniques. She asked me to observe a review lesson on a 'Plants and Seeds' unit she had recently completed. We decided to

concentrate on observing the effectiveness of her questioning techniques rather than the lesson content.

We also decided that I would be in the classroom strictly as an observer. I would not participate in the lesson in any way. We felt that, as many of the children in the room had been former students of mine and because I work with her class two periods every week, the children were familiar with me and comfortable in my presence. We also decided not to use a tape-recorder or videotape so that the children would not be inhibited by them. Maureen and I discussed the most effective way of monitoring and decided on a checklist. I made a checklist and showed it to Maureen. Maureen agreed that it should give us the information we needed.

I positioned myself in the room within the children's immediate sight but slightly separated from the group. As I was within the field of their vision, I would not be causing distraction through children turning to check to see what I was doing. By separating myself slightly from the group, I was implying that I was not participating in the lesson. Maureen reinforced this by telling the children that I was going to watch because I didn't believe that they knew anything about plants and seeds. As we had predicted, outside of an occasional quick glance or smile, the children tended to ignore my presence.

When we first sat down, Maureen allowed the class about a minute of 'wriggle time' before she began to speak. She quickly explained my presence, then went directly into the lesson. She began by giving the children 'fact' questions that they could answer directly from the pictures. The responses were slow to come. Few children volunteered to answer the first few questions. As Maureen continued with the 'fact' questions, the children became more excited and eager to answer.

Maureen then began to inject 'inference questions'. The children were experiencing such success with 'fact questions' that they experienced no trouble in making inferences from the pictures. She then interspersed questions which required the children to form opinions. Again, the children responded freely and confidently. The children began to get restless after about 15 minutes and their attention began to wander. Maureen realized what was happening and quickly ended the lesson.

Looking at the checklist after the observation, my reactions to Maureen's questioning techniques were confirmed. The questions were asked clearly and concisely. The children had full understanding of the type of response that was being elicited. As they understood the questions, they were comfortable and eager to respond.

Maureen's interaction with the children was warm and caring. She listened carefully and respectfully to each response whether the response was correct or incorrect. She encouraged hesitant children by smiling at them, giving verbal encouragement or nodding while the child was speaking. She was careful to ensure that each child had the opportunity to respond at least once during the lesson.

I feel that Maureen has excellent questioning techniques. This includes the variety in the type of questions she asks, the manner in which she uses her voice, the positive reinforcement she employs, the pace of the lesson and the warmth she shows towards the children.

I feel that Maureen's main problem with questioning techniques is that she doesn't recognize her expertise in this area. I would suggest she tape the lessons that use intensive questioning methods and analyse the results for her own benefit.

FOCUSED OBSERVATION

When a pair of teachers have decided on a focus for an observation (e.g. questioning technique), they are often at a loss as to exactly what to look at or for. They may not know, for example, the range of higher-order/lower-order questions. In another situation, they may have decided to look at 'praise' in their classrooms, but when they think more about it they may have some difficulty in describing all the different possible forms of praise. Or again even with a phrase as commonplace as 'effective teaching', what exactly is it that we are looking for? In these situations, it may be helpful to draw on some external resources to help focus the observation. It may be that the teachers who were focusing on 'questioning' would find a form like that illustrated in Figure 7.2 of some help; or the teachers interested in praise may find the lists of effective and ineffective praise illuminating (see Table 7.1); similarly, the teachers who were discussing effective teaching may find the observation schedule, distilled from four works on the subject, a useful research tool (see Table 7.2).

All of these forms, *aide-mémoires* and summaries of research can be of help as long as they are subject to the teacher's own judgement. Problems arise when the checklist controls the focus of the observation, or encourages the observer to become judgemental. This is another situation when Lawrence Stenhouse's (1975: 142) warning that such specifications are to be regarded as intelligent, but not necessarily correct, is apposite. They are there to help focus and refine the teacher's judgement, not supplant it. It should also go without saying that such 'prompts' should be agreed and negotiated beforehand. If the use of criteria are implied in the observation, then they also should be negotiated, shared and understood by all those involved.

FORM 10.6 Questioning techniques

Use: When teacher is asking class or group questions
Purpose: To see if teacher is following principles for good questioning practices

For each question, code the following categories:

Behaviour categories

A *Type of question asked*
1 Academic: Factual. Seeks specific correct response
2 Academic: Opinion. Seeks opinion on a complex issue where there is no clear-cut response
3 Non-academic: Question deals with personal, procedural, or disciplinary matters rather than curriculum

B *Type of response required*
1 Thought question. Student must reason through to a conclusion or explain something at length
2 Fact question. Student must provide fact(s) from memory
3 Choice question. Requires only a yes–no or either–or response

C *Selection of respondent*
1 Names child before asking question
2 Calls on volunteer (after asking question)
3 Calls on non-volunteer (after asking question)

D *Pause (after asking question)*
1 Paused a few seconds before calling on student
2 Failed to pause before calling on student
3 Not applicable; teacher named student before asking question

E *Tone and manner in presenting question*
1 Question presented as challenge or stimulation
2 Question presented matter-of-factly
3 Question presented as threat or test

Record any information relevant to the following:
Multiple Questions. Tally the number of times the teacher:
1 Repeats or rephrases question before calling on anyone   _11_
2 Asks two or more questions at the same time   _0_

Sequence. Were questions integrated into an orderly sequence or did they seem to be random or unrelated?

Teacher seemed to be following sequence given in manual (led up to next history unit).

Did students themselves pose questions?   No

Was there student–student interaction?
How much?   None

When appropriate, did the teacher redirect questions to several students or ask students to evaluate their own or others' responses?   No

Codes

	A	B	C	D	E
1	1	2	2	1	2
2	1	2	2	1	2
3	1	3	2	1	2
4	1	2	2	1	2
5	1	2	2	1	2
6	1	3	2	1	2
7	1	2	2	1	2
8	2	1	2	1	1
9	1	2	2	1	2
10	1	2	2	1	2
11	1	2	2	1	2
12	1	2	2	1	2
13					
14					
15					
16					
17					
18					
19					
20					
21					
22					
23					
24					
25					
26					
27					
28					
29					
30					
31					
32					
33					
34					
35					
36					
37					
38					
39					
40					

Figure 7.2 Questioning techniques (from Good and Brophy 1997).

Table 7.1 Guidelines for effective praise

Effective praise	Ineffective praise
1 Is delivered contingently	1 Is delivered randomly or unsystematically
2 Specifies the particulars of the accomplishment	2 Is restricted to global positive reactions
3 Shows spontaneity, variety and other signs of credibility; suggests clear attention to the student's accomplishment	3 Shows a bland uniformity that suggests a conditioned response made with minimal attention
4 Rewards attainment of specified performance criteria (which can include effort criteria, however)	4 Rewards mere participation, without consideration of performance processes or outcomes
5 Provides information to students about their competence or the value of their accomplishments	5 Provides no information at all or gives students information about their status
6 Orients students towards better appreciation of their own task-related behaviour and thinking about problem-solving	6 Orients students towards comparing themselves with others and thinking about competing
7 Uses students' own prior accomplishments as the context for describing present accomplishments	7 Uses the accomplishments of peers as the context for describing students' present accomplishments
8 Is given in recognition of noteworthy effort or success at difficult (for *this* student) tasks	8 Is given without regard to the effort expended or the meaning of the accomplishment
9 Attributes success to effort and ability, implying that similar successes can be expected in the future	9 Attributes success to ability alone or to external factors such as luck or low task difficulty
10 Fosters endogenous attributions (students believe that they expend effort on the task because they enjoy the task and/or want to develop task-relevant skills)	10 Fosters exogenous attributions (students believe that they expend effort on the task for external reasons – to please the teacher, win a competition or reward, etc.)
11 Focuses students' attention on their own task-relevant behaviour	11 Focuses students' attention on the teacher as an external authority figure who is manipulating them
12 Fosters appreciation of, and desirable attributions about, task-relevant behaviour after the process is completed	12 Intrudes into the ongoing process, distracting attention from task-relevant behaviour

Source: Reproduced with permission from Brophy (1981).

Table 7.2   IQEA Observation schedule relating to features of effective teaching

An effective teacher	Check when observed
achieves eye contact with pupils during lessons	
allows pupil practice after each learning step	
allows short breaks where pupils move about	
allows pupils thinking time	
asks a large number of questions	
attributes ownership of ideas to initiating pupils	
attributes pupils' successes to their efforts	
avoids digressions/ambiguous phrases	
calls pupils by first names	
checks for pupil understanding	
conveys sense of enthusiasm in presentation of tasks	
discourages pupil–pupil verbal abuse	
gets high percentage of correct answers from pupils	
gets pupils to restate answers	
gives clear/detailed instructions/explanations	
gives concrete, varied examples	
gives hints, clues	
gives moderate amount of praise	
gives short review of previous learning	
guides pupils during initial practice	
has brief contacts with individual pupils (maximum 30 seconds)	
has pupils asking questions/initiating verbal interactions	
highlights main points of lesson	
is knowledgeable about subject matter	
monitors pupils' work when necessary	
moves around class and approaches all pupils	
obtains responses from all pupils	
organizes break when pupils' energy wanes	
organizes short transitions between activities	
presents new material in short steps	
provides answers, asking pupils to restate in own words/give other examples	
provides systematic feedback/corrections	

Table 7.2 (*cont'd*)

An effective teacher	Check when observed
rephrases questions	
responds positively to incorrect answers, identifying correct parts	
restates questions	
specifies expected pupil performance on tasks	
specifies what pupils did to achieve success	
teaches with pace	
uses anecdotes, asides relating to task	
uses humour	

Source: Beresford (1998: 85–6).

STRUCTURED OBSERVATION

Although the *aide-mémoires* described in the previous section are helpful in some situations, often all that an observer requires is fairly simple information that can be collected by either using a *tally system* or a *diagram*. I call this approach 'structured observation'.

With a *tally system*, an observer puts down a tally or tick *every time* a particular event occurs, e.g. every time the teacher asks a question or gives praise. The resulting record is factual rather than judgemental and can be made more detailed by basing them on *aide-mémoires* such as those described earlier. The aim of a *diagram* is to produce a record of what happens in the classroom. It records in diagrammatic form a series of classroom interactions. This approach lends itself to a factual or a descriptive record. It should be noted that all of these approaches can fit a wide range of concerns. They can focus on aspects of the teacher's work, pupil-teacher interaction or the work of one or more pupils.

The following examples of structured observation involve both tally systems and diagrams. They were developed by teachers who were interested in gathering data on questioning techniques and on- or off-task behaviour.

Observing questioning techniques

1 *Question distribution*: in Box 7.1 the circles represent pupils. When they answer a question, the number of the question is entered into their circle; blank circles indicate pupils who have not answered a question.
2 *Volunteered and solicited answers*: in Box 7.2 the circles again represent pupils. Use a 'V' for pupils who volunteer answers and an 'A' for those who are asked to answer. Placing a number beside the 'V' or 'A' will indicate the sequence of the questioning (e.g. V1, A2, V3, V4, A5, A6, etc.).

Box 7.1

3 *Teacher response to questions answered*: indicate how the teacher responds to answers by using the following abbreviations. Tally scores as in Box 7.3.

  V = verbal response
 NV = non-verbal response
  + = indicated positive response
  0 = indicated no response
  − = indicated negative response.

Box 7.2

Observing on-task/off-task behaviours

- Identify, by scanning the classroom, all of the students who appear to be off-task every two minutes. Number each scan, using the same number for all pupils who appear to be off-task during that scan. For example, during scan 7, five pupils appeared to be off-task as in Box 7.4.
- Tally on-task/off-task behaviour: list in the off-task column the number of pupils off-task at each scan (say every two minutes). Subtract the

Box 7.3

Question	Response				
	V	NV	+	0	–
1	✓		✓		
2	✓		✓		
3		✓	✓		
4	✓				✓
5		✓		✓	
6	✓		✓		
7	✓		✓		
8	✓			✓	
9		✓	✓		
10		✓		✓	
Totals	6	4	6	3	1

off-task from the class total to determine on-task pupils. Work out the percentages as in Box 7.5.

- Tally observable off-task behaviour by using the following code:

  1 talking not related to task assigned,
  2 doodling,
  3 daydreaming,
  4 wandering around,
  5 working at other tasks,
  6 physically bothering other pupils,
  7 attempting to draw attention,
  8 pencil-sharpener, fountain, washroom,
  9 other.

This observation is easiest to do if you concentrate on a small number of pupils over an extended period of time, rather than trying to observe a whole class at once. During each scan (say every two minutes), observe the off-task behaviour and place the appropriate number in the space. If the student is on-task during the scan, the space is left blank as seen in Box 7.6.

Box 7.4

SYSTEMATIC OBSERVATION

Classroom observations using coding scales are generally appropriate where a range of behaviours, too numerous to record in an open observation and too complex to collect in a structured observation, need to be mapped. Recording the on-task and off-task behaviour of students, *along with their causes,* would require such an approach, as would an audit and categorization of teaching strategies used in a range of lessons.

Box 7.5

Scan	Off-task		On-task	
	Number	%	Number	%
1	4	16	21	84
2	6	24	19	76
3	1	4	24	96
4	0	0	25	100
5	3	12	22	88
6	3	12	22	88
7	6	24	19	76
8	5	20	20	80
9	4	16	21	84
10	4	16	21	84
Total	36		214	
Average		15		85

Box 7.6

Student	Scan										
	1	2	3	4	5	6	7	8	9	10	%
Jeroen	3	4			3			8			40
Jessica	2	2		3	3		4	2	3	2	80
Marloes	6	7			6	6		7			40
David		5	5			5	5		5		50
Dylan	1	1	1	8				8	1		70

Although it may be preferable for teacher-researchers to devise their own observation scales, sometimes they may not have the time, or they may already be familiar with an existing coding scale previously invented. In this section, I will discuss a variety of coding scales that can be utilized in specific situations by teachers, and give a more detailed illustration of one interaction scale – the Flanders Interaction Analysis Categories.

The research approach that relies entirely on the use of observation scales is known as 'systematic classroom observation'. The impetus for coding scales and checklists has come from North America where there is, and has been for some time, a concern for 'scientific' approaches to teaching (Gage 1978). But there is also a strong British tradition of systematic classroom observation; for example, the Oracle Project in primary education, which was the first large-scale study of classroom interaction in Britain (Galton *et al.* 1980).

There are some potential problems in the use of coding or interaction scales. The first problem is that most scales were not designed for use by teachers. Their original intent was as research tools for analysing classrooms. Given the aspirations of this book, however, it is important to stress that these are tools teachers can use to enhance their practice. The teacher-researcher's orientation is always action.

The second difficulty is that each scale represents the author's concept of a situation. One is looking at classrooms through someone else's eyes: their purposes and perceptions could be very different from one's own. It is easy, therefore, to get trapped within the intentions of the researcher who designed the scale. Consequently, it is important for the teacher-researcher to match his or her needs closely to the intent and focus of the scale. In that way, the teacher-researcher can maintain control over the situation.

Third, there is a heavy emphasis on quantitative methods in systematic observation. This frequently results in a conflict between statistical rigour and analytical richness. In my opinion, this inevitably leads to abstraction rather than reflection on (or in) action. This approach often leads away from the classroom rather than into it. To misquote T.S. Eliot, systematic observers may well have the experience, but in so doing they are in danger of losing the meaning.

Because of the 'scientific' bias in this approach it is unsurprising to find that most coding scales available are American in origin. As Galton (1978) comments:

> The obvious starting point for any classification of interaction analysis systems must be *Mirrors for Behaviour* (Simon and Boyer, 1975). The current edition of this anthology contains some 200 observation schedules. Most are American and only two are British. In their collection the observation instruments are classified under eight main headings:
>
> 1 the subject of observation (teacher, pupil),
> 2 the setting under which the instrument is used (subject area),
> 3 the number of targets observed,

4 the coding unit used,
5 the collecting method employed,
6 the number of observers required,
7 the dimensions of the system (affective, cognitive), and
8 the uses reported by the author.

One of the problems with many of the American scales is that they are overly concerned with the formal teaching situation. British researchers have also been developing their own coding scales which, in general, stand in contrast to the American models. Galton (1978) comments again:

> A feature of British research has been the wide variety of different organisational contexts within which classroom observation has been carried out. Much criticism has been directed at American systems because they often seem appropriate only to the more formal type of teaching situation. One of the most interesting features of the British research is the emphasis on observation in informal settings at one extreme and the variety of schedules suitable for use in the microteaching setting for the purpose of evaluating performance in questioning and lecturing skills at the other.

These quotations from Galton (1978) are taken from his book *British Mirrors*, which is a collection of 41 classroom observation systems that are British in origin. The majority of these instruments are junior and secondary school oriented but some are specifically designed for infant or higher education settings. Their target is almost exclusively teachers and pupils, most require only one observer and they are almost exclusively concerned with descriptions of classroom practice. The four major foci of the instruments are: classroom climate, organizational learning, the management and control of routine activities, and knowledge content. In general, they are applicable across all curriculum areas.

One of the earliest coding systems is the Flanders Interaction Analysis Categories (FIAC). Although it may not necessarily be the most effective of the systems available, it is probably the best known. It is widely used and has influenced the design of many other category systems.

FIAC is based on ten analytical categories that reflects Flanders' conceptualization of teacher–pupil verbal interaction (see Table 7.3). Each of the categories has a number, but no scale is implied. In his book *Analysing Teaching Behaviour*, Flanders (1970) described the ten categories in detail, but for our purposes the descriptions given are sufficient. In order to help memorize the categories and make coding easier, one can shorten the descriptions of the categories as shown in Box 7.7.

The procedures for using the Flanders system are quite straightforward. Observers are first trained until they show a high level of agreement

Table 7.3 Flanders Interaction Analysis Categories

Teacher talk

Indirect influence	1	*Accepts feelings*: accepts and clarifies the feeling tone of the student in a non-threatening manner. Feelings may be positive or negative. Predicting and recalling feelings are included
	2	*Praises or encourages*: praises or encourages student action or behaviour. Jokes that release tension, not at the expense of another individual, nodding head or saying 'uh huh?' or 'go on' are included
	3	*Accepts or uses ideas of student*: clarifying, building or developing ideas or suggestions by a student. As teacher brings more of his own ideas into play, shift to category 5
	4	*Asks questions*: asking a question about content or procedure with the intent that a student answer
Direct influence	5	*Lectures*: giving facts or opinions about content or procedures, expressing his own idea; asking rhetorical questions
	6	*Gives directions*: directions, commands or orders with which a student is expected to comply
	7	*Criticizes or justifies authority*: statements, intended to change student behaviour from non-acceptable to acceptable pattern; bawling someone out; stating why the teacher is doing what he is doing, extreme self-reference

Student talk

	8	*Student talk-response*: talk by students in response to teacher. Teacher initiates the contact or solicits student statement
	9	*Student talk-initiation*: talk by students, which they initiate. If 'calling on' student is only to indicate who may talk next, observer must decide whether student wanted to talk. If he did, use this category
	10	*Silence or confusion*: pauses, short periods of silence, and periods of confusion in which communication cannot be understood by the observer

Source: Open University (1976).

with other trained observers. Once they have been trained, they watch a lesson and apply the technique as follows using a coding sheet such as that illustrated in Figure 7.3.

1 Every three seconds the observer writes down the category best describing the verbal behaviour of the teacher and class.
2 The numbers are written in sequence across the data sheet.
3 Each line of the data sheet contains 20 squares, thus representing approximately one minute of time.

Box 7.7

Teacher talk	1	accepts feelings
	2	praise
	3	accepts ideas
	4	question
	5	lecture
	6	command
	7	criticism
Pupil talk	8	solicited
	9	unsolicited
	10	silence

Source: Open University (1976).

4 Separate 'episodes' can be identified by scribbled margin notes, and a new line commenced for a new 'episode'.
5 In a research project, the observer would have a pocket timer designed to give a signal every three seconds, thus reminding him or her to record a tally (a stop-watch or the second hand of a wristwatch can be used).

Two main advantages of the Flanders system are that it is fairly easy to learn and apply, and that the ten categories describe a number of behaviours which many would agree are important, such as the teacher's use of praise and criticism and the pupil's solicited and unsolicited talk. Also, the tallying of events every three seconds enables considerable information to be collected and analysed. There is usually a high agreement between trained observers.

On the other hand, much information is lost, especially non-verbal aspects of communication. In particular, some categories are too broad (e.g. category 4) and others discriminate insufficiently. For example, category 5 does not discriminate between giving information which is correct and that which is incorrect. Category 10 can represent both the silence achieved by an autocrat and the chaos which occurs when a teacher has lost control. Also, there are too few pupil categories, and it is difficult to use in informal classrooms, where two or more members may be talking at once.

For our purposes, FIAC is most appropriately used as a means for gathering classroom data that can then be used as a basis for action. So, for example, if after using FIAC a teacher discovered that he or she was talking too much, then that becomes an identifiable problem upon which action can be taken and monitored by classroom research procedures.

School _____   Teacher _____
Class _____   Subject _____
Date _____   Observer _____
Lesson (1st, 2nd, etc.) _____

TALLY ACROSS

01																		
02																		
03																		
04																		
05																		
06																		
07																		
08																		
09																		
10																		
11																		
12																		
13																		
14																		
15																		
16																		
17																		
18																		
19																		
20																		
21																		
22																		
23																		
24																		
25																		
26																		
27																		
28																		
29																		
30																		

Figure 7.3 FIAC lesson observation sheet (Open University 1976).

Box 7.8

		Category number tallied by observer
Teacher:	'Look at the map on page 60'	6 (command)
Teacher:	'What is the country coloured green?'	4 (question)
	three-second pause	10 (silence)
Pupil:	'I think it's Finland, but I'm not sure.'	8 (solicited pupil talk)

Data sheet entry
(minute 12 of the lesson)

12	6	4	10	8

Source: Open University (1976).

A simple example illustrates the first few seconds of an exchange occurring in the twelfth minute of a lesson.

The teacher tells children to look at a map on page 60 of their books and asks the name of the country coloured green. There is a short pause and then a child replied. The text of this exchange and the data sheet would look like that shown in Box 7.8.

FURTHER READING

Rob Walker's (1989) *Doing Research* and Colin Hook's (1981) *Studying Classrooms* both contain exemplary and sound advice on methods of classroom observation that are sympathetic to the theme of this book. Walker and Adelman (1990) also provide useful information on classroom observation. Hitchcock and Hughes (1995), in their *Research and the Teacher*, provide extensive advice but from a more traditional perspective. Good and Brophy's (1997) *Looking in Classrooms* contains many schedules for assessing classroom behaviour; this book is an important resource for teacher-researchers, as it provides a range of material on teaching skills and ways of measuring their impact in the classroom. Sara Delamont's (1983) *Interaction in the Classroom* is a balanced and introductory account of the domain of classroom observation research. Paul Croll's (1997) *Systematic Classroom Observation* contains a fairly sustained argument for the centrality of systematic observation in quantitative research. This book also provides a detailed introduction to the large-scale *Oracle* and *One in Five* classroom interaction research studies. The approach taken in this book, however, tends to lead away from the classroom rather than into it, and Croll over-emphasizes, in my opinion, the distinction between teachers and researchers rather than the benefits of collaboration between them. In the same tradition, the two collections of classroom observation scales by Simon and Boyer (1975) and Galton (1978) are primary resources for teacher-researchers wanting examples of coding scales. Critiques of these various approaches to classroom interaction and observation are to be found in Sara Delamont's (1984) *Readings on Interaction in the Classroom* and Martin Hammersley's (1993) *Controversies in Classroom Research*. John Beresford (1998), in his *Collecting Information for School Improvement*, provides a range of instruments for school-based and classroom research, as well as useful hints on how to administer them.

CHAPTER 8

Data gathering

In this chapter, I discuss a variety of techniques other than observation that teachers can use to gather information about their teaching. I will observe a similar format in discussing each of the approaches: the technique will briefly be described, advantages and disadvantages will be considered, appropriate uses will be stated and an example of the technique in practice will be given. At the end of the chapter, I will present a taxonomy of teacher research methods.

The Ford Teaching Project (Elliott and Adelman 1976) in general, and the booklet *Ways of Doing Research in One's Own Classroom* (Bowen *et al.* n.d.) in particular, provided the inspiration for this chapter. The idea for the boxes illustrating the advantages/disadvantages of the data collection methods came from the appendix of *Ways of Doing Research in One's Own Classroom* and a number of the points made there are reproduced here verbatim. Also, all the methods of data collection mentioned below, with the exception of sociometry, were used by the Ford Teaching Project. Once again I am very grateful to the Ford Teaching Project for allowing me to use their material in this chapter.

Before describing these methods in more detail, two caveats have to be entered. The first is that describing the techniques individually may give a false impression of orderliness and discreteness. In practice, these techniques are more often than not used eclectically and in combination. Second, we need to remember the criteria established earlier which cautioned that the method employed should not be too demanding on the teacher's time.

FIELD NOTES

Keeping field notes is a way of reporting observations, reflections and reactions to classroom problems. Ideally, they should be written as soon as possible after a lesson, but can be based on impressionistic jottings made during a lesson. The greater the time-lapse between the event and recording it, the more difficult it becomes to reconstruct problems and responses accurately and retain conscious awareness of one's original thinking. Many teachers I know keep a notebook open on their desk or keep a space in their daybooks for jotting down notes as the lesson and the day progresses. Keeping a record in this way is not very time-consuming and provides surprisingly frank information that is built up over time. They also provide a fascinating biographical record of our development as teachers.

Field notes can be of a number of different types. They can be 'issue-oriented' insofar as the observations focus on a particular aspect of one's teaching or classroom behaviour and constitute an on-going record. On the other hand, they can reflect general impressions of the classroom, its climate or incidental events. Field notes can also be used to provide case study material of a particular child. This information should be descriptive rather than speculative, so that a broad picture amenable to interpretation can be built up.

The main advantages and disadvantages of field notes are listed in point form in Box 8.1.

Box 8.1

Advantages	Disadvantages
• Very simple to keep; no outsider needed	• Need to fall back on aids such as question analysis sheets, tapes and transcripts for specific information
• Provide good on-going record; used as a diary they give good continuity	• Conversation impossible to record by field notes
• First-hand information can be studied conveniently in teacher's own time	• Notebook works with small groups but not with a full class
• Acts as an *aide-mémoire*	• Initially time-consuming
• Helps to relate incidents, explore emerging trends	• Can be highly subjective
• Very useful if teacher intends to write a case study	

Four uses of field notes in classroom research are:

1 They can focus on a particular issue or teaching behaviour over a period of time.
2 They can reflect general impressions of the classroom and its climate.
3 They can provide an on-going description of an individual child that is amenable to interpretation and use in case study.
4 They can record our development as teachers.

In this example Ian uses field notes to build up a picture of the work ethic in a low academic set of 12–13-year-olds.

I started making observations, keeping a note pad on the desk. I chose not to take a particular focus. After making initial observations on movement, posture and seating arrangements, and after some interviews of a general nature concerning the pupil's attitudes to the teaching of language and the organization into sets that the pupils had to submit to, a picture of the work ethic of a low academic set was gradually built up.

For each distinct activity that goes on in the English language lesson (story writing, grammar skills, etc.), the working environments and climates are different. In language work, for example, there is always an initial rush to complete *one* card – the minimum requirement. When this is completed, although another card is often collected, intensive work ceases and chatting about the weekend, with some desultory work, is the norm (the lesson is first period Monday). This ritualized behaviour has the function of reaffirming certain social groups, and talk is, interestingly enough, voluntarily kept to quite a quiet level. The various friendship groups have distinct topics of conversation which don't vary much over the year. Changes to the seating, which I have tried, cause a much higher level of noise. All the other English activities – each one has one lesson a week – have different structures and patterns of social interaction, attitudes and noise levels which have built up over time.

I noted that the pattern of work throughout the term – and the year – is affected by traditional school rituals. The arrangement of pupils into sets is reviewed at the end of each term and this ritual always influences work rate and conversation:

Girl: You 'eard about moving up yet, sir?
Teacher: No, I've been asked to make three recommendations to go up and down. Mr . . . will make the decision. [chorus of inquiries]

Girl: Shut up you – you're thick. If you move, it'll be down. I
          hope I move up – we do no work in 'ere. 'Alf of 'em can't
          even write (looking at the boys). (Cheers from boys)

The low status of the set is always a factor in the pupils' perceptions
of their ability and in their attitude to work.

[This example is taken from a series of teacher-researcher reports on children's thinking in Hull *et al.* (1985). At a later date, the teacher could have
used notes like this as 'evidence' in discussions with his students about
their progress and aspirations.]

AUDIOTAPE RECORDING

Audiotape recording is one of the most popular teacher research methods.
Transcripts are excellent for those situations where teachers require a very
specific and accurate record of a limited aspect of their teaching, or of a
particular interaction, say between a specific teacher and child or between
two children. An increasing number of teachers are using audiotape as
one further way of gathering data to support other forms of assessment,
albeit on an incidental basis. Also, simply playing back tapes of one's
teaching can be very illuminating and provide useful starting points for
further investigation. Having a tape deck in one's car is a great asset for
doing this.

    Playing back tapes or making transcripts can be very time-
consuming and expensive, however, unless the method is used judici-
ously. The Ford Teaching Project teachers and staff were very enthusiastic
about this method, but they did have secretarial support for making transcripts. Most teachers do not, and for that reason I advise against it as a
broad-spectrum diagnostic tool.

    On the practical side, the use of the tape-recorder requires some
technical knowledge, so make certain you can use it before taking it into
class and that the batteries are charged! It is important when recording to
ensure that the microphone is picking up what is intended, and this also
may require practice. Pupils often find the presence of a tape-recorder in
the class disturbing and have to be introduced to the technique over time.
Always check with the pupils and other teachers or adults that they do not
mind you recording the conversation or discussion.

    The main advantages and disadvantages of the audiotape recorder
are listed in point form in Box 8.2. Three uses of the tape-recorder in
classroom research are:

Box 8.2

Advantages	Disadvantages
• Very successfully monitors all conversations within range of the recorder	• Nothing visual – does not record silent activities
• Provides ample material with great ease	• Transcription largely prohibitive because of expense and time involved
• Versatility – can be transported or left with a group	• Masses of material may provide little relevant information
• Records personality developments	• Can disturb pupils because of its novelty; can be inhibiting
• Can trace development of a group's activities	• Continuity can be disturbed by the practical problems of operating
• Can support classroom assessment	

1 As a general diagnostic tool for identifying aspects of one's teaching.
2 For providing detailed evidence on specific aspects of teaching through the use of transcripts.
3 As an additional source of evidence for classroom assessment.

> **In this example Val uses an audiotape-recorder as an aid to understanding children's thinking in relation to sketch maps in geography.**
>
> The class (of very bright 11-year-olds) was arranged in groups of four or five pupils and each group was given copies of the four maps and asked to discuss them and decide which they thought was 'best'. I only had access to one tape-recorder and was only able therefore to record one discussion. When I listened to the tape, I realized that discussion clearly had potential as a research tool and that this strategy for gaining access to pupils' critical thinking was worth repeating. Pupils were realistic in their criticisms and were to some extent impersonal. The discussion helped me to see what criteria they were using and how the range of their considerations might be extended.
>
> In my next attempt . . . (there was only one tape-recorder available), there were several groups responding to the maps, so each group chose a leader and he or she gave a report to the class at the end of the discussion and it was the final reports that were

taped. Some of the spontaneity of the original discussion was lost, but nevertheless some interesting points emerged.

It seemed that the brighter pupils were more methodical and precise in their criticism:

Simon: Our verdict on map 1 was that a ruler could have been used and some of the buildings had doors missing and that there wasn't any scale . . . title, key or north direction.
Map 3 – it's a drawing, it's not a map.
Map 4 – that's quite good, that's more of a map, they have got a key and direction and a suitable title.

Sarah: We thought map 1 wasn't very good because the writing is too small.
Map 3 wasn't very good – too artistic.

Valerie: Map 2 was the best because it showed all the roads and railways and bridges.

[This example is taken from a series of teacher-researcher reports on children's thinking in Hull *et al.* (1985). The teacher was subsequently able to use this information to revise the sketch maps; the discussions also helped her adapt her teaching style with more able pupils.]

PUPIL DIARIES

It is common practice in many schools for pupils to keep a daily log. This is also a quick way of obtaining information, as teachers normally check pupil diaries as a matter of course. Also, pupil diaries provide an interesting contrast to the field notes kept by the teacher on the same topic. Once the pupils have been taken into the teacher's confidence and are aware of the teacher's concern to research his or her teaching, then these diaries are an excellent way of obtaining honest feedback, particularly when the pupils retain the right to decide whether the teacher has access to the diary. The teacher can use pupil diaries as feedback on a particular teaching episode, or to gain an indication of the general class climate, or to assess the progress of an individual pupil. When pupils feel comfortable with the approach, they may feel free to write about other teachers and aspects of the school. Sometimes the ethical issues raised by this may be difficult to resolve, particularly when the use of pupil diaries is not commonplace in the school.

The main advantages and disadvantages of pupil diaries are listed in point form in Box 8.3. Three uses of pupil diaries in classroom research are:

1 they provide a pupil perspective on a teaching episode
2 they provide data on the general climate of the classroom, and
3 they provide information for triangulation.

Box 8.3

Advantages	Disadvantages
• Provides feedback from pupil's perspective • Can be either focused on a specific training episode or related to the general classroom climate • Can be part of a lesson • Can help in identifying individual pupil problems • Involves pupil in improving the quality of the class • Provides a basis for triangulation	• May not be an established practice in the school • Difficult for younger children to record their thoughts and feelings • Pupils may be inhibited in discussing their feelings with the teacher • Pupil's accounts are obviously subjective • May raise ethical dilemmas

In this example Judy is using pupil diaries as part of her strategy for reorganizing her maths class.

I used the diaries mainly as immediate feedback for myself and as an aid in monitoring the daily progress of the students. The following are samples of information that I gathered from the various student diaries during a four-week period:

1 There were explanations as to why they hadn't completed a number of assignments for my substitute while I was at a convention.
2 Throughout the four weeks the students used the logs to tell me when they were having trouble with an assignment and to ask to see me the next day for help.
3 A number of students suggested that I put in a centre containing mazes and logic puzzles that they could go to when they had completed all their assignments.
4 Occasionally, a pupil would ask me to change their seating arrangement as they weren't able to work near a certain person.
5 Many of them began to use the log to establish a private conversation between us.
6 I used the logs to indicate when I was disappointed in a student's performance or behaviour and to question them about it. I found that they were more open since they weren't put on the spot in front of their classmates.

7 Some of them mentioned when they felt I had let the noise level get too high or when they had been able to do more than usual because it had been exceptionally quiet.

8 They pointed out when they had wasted time waiting for me to get their books marked so they could finish off their corrections.

9 I found it especially helped me monitor the progress of my less assertive students.

10 The students would indicate when they felt I had given too heavy a workload for the week.

11 Students twice pointed out that they had come to me for assistance and I had been too busy to help them.

I felt that these logs were one of the most valuable aspects of my research project. They weren't always relevant to my actual research, but the personal contact I managed to establish with each of my students was of more importance to me than keeping them on target concerning their work in the maths programme.

INTERVIEWS

Interviewing in classroom research can take four forms: it can occur between teacher and pupil, observer and pupil, pupil and pupil and, occasionally, teacher and observer. This latter activity, however, normally occurs as a consequence of peer observation (see Chapters 6 and 7). Because teacher–pupil interviews are very time-consuming, it may be more profitable to devote that time to general classroom meetings, and only talk individually with pupils (for research purposes) when a specific instance warrants it. On the other hand, individual interviews are often very productive sources of information for a participant observer who wants to verify observations he or she has previously made. Like other researchers, however, I increasingly find group interviews with three or four students the most productive. Far from inhibiting each other, the individuals 'spark' themselves into sensitive and perceptive discussion. I also find it helpful to tape-record my summary of the discussion with the students at the end of the interview. This enables them to correct or amplify my interpretation and provides me with a brief and succinct account of the interview that can easily be transcribed.

Pupil–pupil interviews can provide rich sources of data, particularly if the pupil interviewer keeps to an interview schedule prepared by the teacher. It is a good idea to tape-record these individual interviews for future reference, particularly if the encounters are relatively short.

Walker and Adelman (1990) make a number of points about effective interviewing:

1 Be a sympathetic, interested and attentive listener, without taking an active conservative role; this is a way of conveying that you value and appreciate the child's opinion.

2 Be neutral with respect to subject matter. Do not express your own opinions either on the subjects being discussed by the children or on the children's ideas about these subjects, and be especially careful not to betray feelings of surprise or disapproval at what the child knows.

3 Your own sense of ease is also important. If you feel hesitant or hurried, the students will sense this feeling and behave accordingly.

4 The students may also be fearful that they will expose an attitude or idea that you don't think is correct. Reassure along the lines of 'Your opinions are important to me. All I want to know is what you think – this isn't a test and there isn't any one answer to the questions I want to ask.'

5 Specifically we suggest that you:
  • phrase questions similarly each time,
  • keep the outline of interview questions before you, and
  • be prepared to reword a question if it is not understood or if the answer is vague and too general. Sometimes it is hard not to give an 'answer' to the question in the process of rewording it.

The main advantages and disadvantages of interviewing are listed in point form in Boxes 8.4 (a–c).

Box 8.4(a) Teacher/pupil (individually or in groups of three or four)

Advantages	Disadvantages
• Teacher in direct contact with pupil • Pupil(s) familiar with teacher, therefore more at ease • Teacher able to seek information he or she wants directly and not through a ream of irrelevant information • Can be done in lesson time or outside the class • Can follow up problems immediately when they arise and get information while minds are still fresh	• Time-consuming • May be carried out with some form of recording equipment, with attendant disadvantages • Frequently difficult to get younger children to explain their thoughts and feelings

Box 8.4(b) Observer/pupil (individually or in groups of three or four)

Advantages	Disadvantages
• Leaves teacher free as the interviewer discovers initial information from the pupil(s) • Pupil(s) frequently more candid with the outsider than with class teacher or teacher from within the school • Outsider is likely to be more objective • Outsider can focus the information provided along predetermined lines of investigation	• Pupil(s) unfamiliar with observer may be reluctant to divulge relevant information • Mutual uncertainty • If the teacher is the primary agent in the research, then he or she will get his or her information secondhand and subject to the biases of the interviewer • The whole set up is time-consuming as information goes from pupil(s) to interviewer to teacher • Difficult to obtain a skilled outsider

Box 8.4(c) Pupil/pupil

Advantages	Disadvantages
• Pupils may be more candid with each other • Leaves teacher free • Can occur during lesson time • May produce unanticipated/unusual perspectives	• Pupils may find the activity too unfamiliar • May encourage disruption • Has to be recorded and played to teacher

Three uses of the interview in classroom research are:

• to focus on a specific aspect of teaching or classroom life in detail,
• teacher–pupil classroom discussion can provide general diagnostic information, and
• to improve the classroom climate.

This example contains extracts from a conversation between three Year 9 students (S) at the Sanders Draper School, Havering, Mel Ainscow (MA), David Hargreaves (DHH) and myself (DH). Sanders Draper was involved in the 'Improving the Quality of Education for All' school improvement project. The purpose of the discussion was to assess how far the school's development priority 'Resource Based Learning' had affected students' perceptions of the way they were taught and learned. We used this information in feedback to staff, who in turn incorporated it in their own developmental work. I have included such an extended illustration partly for its intrinsic interest, but also to show how classroom research can support whole school development and to illustrate the power of the group interview.

DH: What is it like to learn in this school?

S: It's changed now that we are able to use the library more, we are now using more visual/audio type stuff, videos, rather than just learning out of a textbook.

S: Also teachers tell you to get on with it, rather than them telling you what to do. You can come in here (the library), you find out all the information and you can say to a teacher I want to do this and that, and they say alright then.

S: Well we are more tending to get into things like, in maths for example, we tend to go into our own investigations where we can take a problem and we investigate it in our own way.

DH: Tell me a bit about how you actually find the information.

S: Well, if you find a book, look through the subject index, or there is a disk thing on the computer, it's got all newspaper things, you put the disk in and you say what subjects you want to find out about, type it in and it comes up with all the different things in the subjects. You choose what you want. There is also an encyclopaedia list on the computer.

DH: What happens when you've done all this and got some information on the subject you are dealing with, say four or five bits of information – what do you do then?

S: We either make it into like a folder of work, put it into graphs, or sometimes we get the chance to make a play out of it, but there is still a certain amount of written work to record it all. Things like – they'll tell a certain amount of detail. Like in science they were telling us about disease and then we had to write a newspaper report about it, so used the pictures.

DH: What happens if you get into the situation where you find that one bit of information disagrees with another piece of information. How do you make a decision?

S: Usually you put both of the arguments, both for and against, or you decide which you think, but explain that there are other sides to the idea. Put down what you thought what was right and what was wrong. Put both sides down.

MA: That's quite demanding, do some students struggle with that?

S: It depends if you are looking through hundreds of encyclopaedias for the one thing you are looking for; otherwise you might as well watch it on the video if you are looking for something about the Third Reich, see if they've got a video about it. That's easier. There will always be people who work at different speeds, are capable of different things. When we do learning in our own way, then it is better because they are not trying to keep up with the top students in the class.

DHH: You have given me the impression that this new style of learning, your relationship with the teacher is different.

S: Well it is in some ways because there are some teachers who are sitting there and want to teach you everything on the line, but there are others who think it best for us to work down here (in the library).

DHH: But is it? Is it best for you?

S: Yes, I think it is. I prefer it anyway. You are at your own pace. Not like a teacher dictating to you and you just sitting there with your mouth open.

DH: Some people say that the real way to be taught is to write down lots of notes, do exercises from the book.

S: But the two ways compensate each other. You learn at your own pace and then answer the questions from the book. Then you remember it, take it in rather than just taking notes. You sort of construct it your own way. No real way of learning, different people find it easier to do different things, so I don't think anyone can say it is a lot better to work out of a textbook or it is a lot better to watch a video.

DHH: If I understand you correctly when you take notes, you are not really learning anything.

S: You learn about half of it but if you are in control of your own learning, you are doing it the way you want to do it, you actually want to learn about it, you are taking it in, and remembering more because you are doing it your way.

[*The students then showed us some examples of work.*]

MA: Who produced this?

S: I decided to do it on a computer at home, then it would be easier to read.

MA: So this in a sense summarizes all the research that you did, you've put it into your own words and made an information sheet.

S: Yes, that's what they said, do it like a magazine article, then it comes out in your own words. More likely to remember something that way.

DH: You have been in the school now for three years, do you think there has been a change in the way that teachers teach over those three years?

S: (Since the new Head arrived) the school has got more disciplined.

DH: More disciplined in the school, but at the same time a more open approach to teaching and learning?

S: Well we've been given the chance to like express ourselves, but because of that we've had to go by their rules.

DH: So there is a good response to this more open way.

S: Yes, you've got the responsibility of getting on with what you want to do, you've got to do it even if the teacher isn't watching you. It sort of works two ways, you respect the school rules and they'll respect you, they are trusting you to work on your own.

DHH: Somebody might say, from outside, that you might choose a very slow pace for yourself and the job of the teacher is to make you go at a faster pace. What do you say to that?

S: Well the teachers would like say to you, I don't think you have done enough work. If you have only done a couple of sentences of work for your whole project, they will like give you a detention, or a series of detentions, or something like that. That will teach you to work more rather than at a faster pace.

S: You will always have to do a certain amount of work, you will never give in one sheet of work for a project and it will be OK. That's never going to be told OK so that's your pace then.

DHH: So you are not going to get away with that sort of thing.

S: No.

DH: So that is an example of the rules on the one hand and the flexibility on the other.

S: Yes.

DHH: So it is tough in some ways but not in others.

S: Yes.

S: It's like the correct balance between lenience and strictness. No good coming in one day and doing a little work and then

saying that's enough, then coming in the next day and doing
nothing, you have to try to do as much work as possible on
both days.

[*We were then shown another piece of work.*]

DHH: Did you change your mind on anything when you were
      writing.
S: Yeah I did actually. At first I thought the approach was all
      wrong and it should never be allowed. When I started
      researching into it and found out things, there are fors and
      against. I really decided that it was a matter of individuals
      really, so I put that in there. For and against, and then my
      own views.
DHH: It has a terrific ending to it. You went through the arguments,
      then you made your own mind up personally at the end, and
      then it ends 'then I hope you've decided what *you* think' – the
      reader is asked to decide for himself, or herself.
S: Well really you've got to decide for yourself. There is no one
      who can say that one thing is right and one thing is wrong,
      it's a matter of your own decision.

VIDEOTAPE RECORDER AND DIGITAL CAMERA

The videotape recorder is increasingly being used by teachers as a means of
gathering general information about their teaching. It allows the teacher to
observe many facets of his or her teaching quickly, and provides heuristic
and accurate information for diagnosis. After this, the teacher may wish to
use a different method to examine specific aspects of his or her teaching.

Many of the teacher-researchers I know use the video on an inter-
mittent but regular basis to enable them to keep in touch with their teaching. If an observer or student can be used to operate the videotape recorder,
then more attention can be paid to specific teaching episodes (identified
beforehand) or the reaction of particular students.

The main advantages and disadvantages of the videotape recorder
are listed in point form in Box 8.5a. Three uses of videotape recorders in
classroom research are:

1 for obtaining visual material of the total teaching situation,
2 acting as an aid to diagnosis, and
3 as a means of examining in detail a specific teaching episode.

Photographs, and the more recent use of the digital camera, are
useful ways of recording critical incidents in classrooms or of illustrating

Box 8.5(a) (Videotape recorder)

Advantages	Disadvantages
• Enables all situations to be constantly reviewed • Origin of problems can be diagnosed • Behavioural patterns of teacher and pupils can be seen • Patterns of progress over long periods can be clearly charted	• Can be very conspicuous and distracting • If camera is directed by operator, it will only record that which he or she deems to be of importance; operator acts as editor

Box 8.5(b) (Digital camera)

Advantages	Disadvantages
• Advantage may be obtained by looking at images of kids working, or at end products of their work, and as a stimulus for discussion • As an instrument which helps you get observation and comment from other teachers who were not present at the time	• Shows isolated situations; difficulty of being in the right place at the right time; concentrates on small groups and individuals, not classes; records nothing in depth • Images may not truly depict activities of the children, if photographer is selective

particular teaching episodes. They can also be used to support other forms of data gathering (e.g. interviews or field notes) or as a means for providing reference points for interviews or discussions.

The main advantages and disadvantages of photographs and digital photography are listed in point form in Box 8.5b.

> **In this example I describe the first experience Geoff, a student on one of my in-service courses, had with the videotape recorder.**
>
> Geoff is a deputy head teacher in a special school. His pupils face many learning challenges, but the expectation is that they will

eventually be able to cope by themselves in some limited way. To give his pupils that basic level of life-skill is Geoff's main goal. Geoff used the videotape recorder to examine his teaching and to try and find an answer to the question 'why is everything so time-consuming?'.

Geoff decided to video the morning session from 9:30 to 10:15, which was the most structured and high energy time of the day. During the lesson, the nursery nurse was also involved in the class. Before videoing, Geoff identified a series of topics on which he wanted to get information:

- maximum time worked by each pupil,
- time wasted by each pupil,
- time unavoidably lost,
- time to be spent with each pupil, and
- number of tasks accomplished in the 45-minute session by each pupil.

The videotaping session went well. Geoff had had the camera in his room for a few days, so the pupils were used to having it around. With a wide-angle lens he was able to capture all the activity in the class. Geoff then began reviewing the tape. Besides gathering data on the points above, he also detailed the following:

- amount of time he spent out of the class on administrative duties,
- the number of times he praised/reprimanded a pupil,
- how long the pupils were left unsupervised,
- time spent by nursery nurse with each pupil, and
- pupil's reaction to attention.

Geoff then analysed the tape for each pupil and produced a detailed analysis of how individual lessons were spent. From this information Geoff was able to derive a number of hypotheses concerning the class and set up a programme for utilizing the time more effectively.

QUESTIONNAIRES

Questionnaires that ask specific questions about aspects of the classroom, curriculum or teaching method are a quick and simple way of obtaining broad and rich information from pupils. It is important, however, particularly in the primary grades, to be relatively unsophisticated in the structuring of the questions. Condense the usual 5-point scale to two or three responses, keep the questions simple, and use the basic 'what did you like best', 'what

Figure 8.1

Box 8.6

Advantages	Disadvantages

• Easy to administer; quick to fill in
• Easy to follow up
 	
• Provides direct comparison of groups and individuals
• Provides feedback on:
  – attitudes
  – adequacy of resources
  – adequacy of teacher help
  – preparation for next session
  – conclusions at end of term
• Data are quantifiable
	• Analysis is time-consuming
	• Extensive preparation to get clear and relevant questions
	• Difficult to get questions that explore in depth
	• Effectiveness depends very much on reading ability and comprehension of the child
	• Children may be fearful of answering candidly
	• Children will try to produce 'right' answers

did you like least', 'what would you do differently' type of open-ended question.

With younger (and older) pupils it is often more profitable to use a happy face as the criterion response to questions as in Figure 8.1. More imaginatively, cartoon pictures can be used, as in Figure 8.2 – the possibilities are endless!

The main advantages and disadvantages of the questionnaire are listed in point form in Box 8.6. The main use of the questionnaire in class-room research is to obtain quantitative responses to specific predetermined questions. Examples of questionnaires are given in Figures 8.2 and 8.3.

SOCIOMETRY

Sociometric analysis or sociometry is a technique used to measure the emotional structure of a group. As a diagnostic instrument, sociometry's purpose is to highlight the feelings of attraction, indifference and rejection that occur within a group and between its members. The approach has

Figure 8.2 Reading attitude survey.

Inquiry/discovery follow-up questionnaire
Please put a ring round the answer you wish to give to each question. If you are not sure ring the nearest to what you think.

1	How much of the lesson did you enjoy?	All of it/Some of it/None
2	How much do you think you learnt?	Nothing/Something/A lot
3	How much did you understand?	Most of it/Some of it/Nothing
4	Could you find the books, information, equipment you needed?	None/Some of it/Most of it
5	Did other people help you?	A lot/A little/Not at all
6	Did other people stop you working?	A lot/Sometimes/Not at all
7	Did the teacher help you	Enough/Not enough
8	Did the lesson last	Long enough/Too long/Not long enough
9	Was the lesson	Boring/Interesting
10	Did you need anything you could not find?	Yes/No
11	Where did you get help from?	Teacher/Group/Someone else
12	Did you find this work	Easy/Hard/Just about right
13	Write down anything which made it hard for you to learn	
14	Write down anything you particularly enjoyed about this lesson	

Figure 8.3 A sample questionnaire designed by Roger Pols. Reproduced with permission from Bowen *et al.* (n.d.).

obvious applications to classrooms where teachers want to discover the social structure of the class for research and other purposes. The most important 'other purpose' is to identify pupils who are socially isolated in order to take remedial action.

Before administering a sociometric test, it is important to ensure that the pupils know each other fairly well, that confidentiality is established, and that action be taken as a consequence. Sociometry in this sense is a dynamic process that can lead to improvement in children's attitudes and relationships and the general enhancement of a classroom climate.

Congdon (1978: 6) describes a method for administering the sociometric test:

> Each child is handed a slip of blank paper and told to write his name at the top. Some teachers prefer to have the names of all pupils in the class written on the blackboard. It is always advisable to write up the names of any pupils who are absent. The test should be meaningful to the pupils. So, for example, the context of the test could be a project. After deciding on a project the pupils could be told that they will be allowed to work in groups and that the groups would be made up according to their own choices.

On the left hand side of the sheet the pupils are asked to write the name of the person with whom they would most like to work in a group. Underneath they are asked to write the name of the one they would like next best, then the next and so on. They can be told to write as many names as they wish or none at all. The pupil is then asked to turn over the sheet and again down the left hand side of the page to write the names of any children with whom they do not wish to work. The teacher again tells them that they may write as many names as they wish or none at all. And what is more important she tells them that the names will be known only to herself, i.e. the choices are made privately and no pupil should be told either who chose him or how many choices he received. In this way no one's feelings are hurt.

After the test has been administered, the pupil choices are analysed to establish the structure of relationships within the class. The best known and easiest understood method of doing this is the sociogram. Congdon (1978: 7) continues to describe how a sociogram is constructed:

> In drawing a sociogram it is often useful to begin with the most chosen pupil and add the symbols for any pupils who reciprocate his or her choices. Next, pupils who have mutual choices with this group can be added. When these have been exhausted then a fresh group can be drawn up starting with the next most highly-chosen pupil and so on. The sociogram can be completed by filling in the unreciprocated choices.

Figure 8.4 is an example of a sociogram for a group of eight individuals with the symbols most commonly used marked on it.

Clearly, in Figure 8.4 pupils E, F and H are unpopular and this information encourages the teacher to act to remedy this situation; action that can also be monitored through other classroom research techniques. The sociogram is a useful method for teacher-researchers who wish to explore

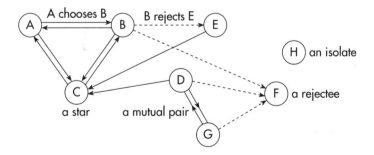

Figure 8.4 Example of a sociogram.

Box 8.7

Advantages	Disadvantages
• Simple way to discover social relationships in class • Provides guide to action • Can be integrated into class activity	• Possibility of compounding the isolation of some pupils

the social structure of their class and the relationships between pupils. It also provides a starting point for action and further research. As sociometry emphasizes the class as a group, parallel efforts could focus on the perspectives of individual children, using, for example, self-concept inventories.

The major advantages and disadvantages of sociometry are listed in point form in Box 8.7. The main use of sociometry in classroom research is to disclose the social structure of the class.

> **In this example Ann was using a behaviour modification 'game' to improve the level of assignment completion in her maths class.**
>
> Since I had scruples about such a game causing social rejection of the target pupils, a sociogram was done before and after the experiment. Pupils were each asked to name three children they would like to sit next to during art lessons or storytime. It was stressed that this would be a non-academic, non-competitive time. The first choices were assigned three points, the second two points and the third one point. Points were totalled and the results entered on a graph.
>
> Pre- and post-use of the sociogram showed that the popularity of the target pupils was not detrimentally affected by the game. None of them were social isolates but they all fell into the lower half of the class.

DOCUMENTARY EVIDENCE

Documents (memos, letters, position papers, examination papers, newspaper clippings, etc.) surrounding a curriculum or other educational concern can illuminate rationale and purpose in interesting ways. The use of such material can provide background information and understanding of issues that would not otherwise be available.

Box 8.8

Advantages	Disadvantages
• Illuminate issues surrounding a curriculum or teaching method • Provide context, background and understanding • Provide an easy way of obtaining other people's perceptions	• Obtaining documents can be time-consuming • Certain documents may be difficult to obtain • Certain persons may be unwilling to share 'confidential' documents

The main advantages and disadvantages of documentary evidence are listed in point form in Box 8.8. The main use of documents in classroom research is that they provide a context for understanding a particular curriculum or teaching method.

In this example Gill used documents to understand the nature of the art curriculum.

During her work for a postgraduate degree, Gill, an art teacher, examined some of the influences on the art curriculum. Her reason for doing this was largely personal: increasingly she was feeling a tension between her aspirations for art teaching and the general approach to the art curriculum that she was being encouraged to adopt. Gill's approach to the teaching of art was essentially child-centred. She has a commitment to developing a pupil's artistic talents and her teaching style and the activities she set her pupils were designed to achieve this goal. Her investigation involved examining a range of past papers and examiners' comments. To her chagrin, she found that the art curriculum in general was influenced not by pupil achievement or aspirations but more by the examiners' (rather traditional) comments. This discovery served at least to explain her tension. It also encouraged her to develop a scheme of work in painting for younger pupils and propose alternative syllabi for examination pupils that integrated her own ideas on art teaching with the more traditional approach.

CASE STUDY

The case study is a relatively formal analysis of an aspect of classroom life. Some teachers may wish to produce case studies for a university course

Box 8.9

Advantages	Disadvantages
• A relatively simple way of plotting the progress of a course or a pupil's or group's reaction to teaching methods • Information yielded by case studies will tend to give a more accurate and representative picture than will any one of the research methods detailed above; case studies draw on data gathered by many methods	• In order for the case study to be of value it must be fairly exhaustive; this means that it will be time-consuming in its preparation and its writing • Feedback available to teacher only after considerable lapse of time

they are taking or as research towards a higher degree. These situations apart, it is unlikely that teachers will devote time to producing a formal case report of their teacher-researcher efforts every time they undertake a project. (For a more detailed discussion of case study research see Stake 1995.)

The main advantages and disadvantages of the case study are listed in point form in Box 8.10. The main use of the case study in classroom research is that it provides a relatively formal and fairly definitive analysis of a specific aspect of teaching behaviour or classroom life. Examples of teacher research case studies are given in Chapters 2 and 6.

MAPPING THE 'PROCESS OF CHANGE' IN SCHOOLS

The final data gathering method refers to a battery of techniques rather than a single approach, so will therefore be described a little differently from the others. During our programme of research and development into school improvement, we have come to recognize that traditional research methods are sometimes too cumbersome and time-consuming in disclosing the intricacies of the change process. We felt that there was room for new, more user-friendly yet penetrating techniques for investigating and measuring the complex processes and relationships involved in school change. With a grant from the ESRC we developed six new techniques for mapping the process of change in schools. (A comprehensive description, with advice on administration, of the techniques is found in the manual produced as a result of the research *Mapping Change in Schools: The Cambridge Manual of Research Techniques* (Cambridge University 1994) and in a paper by Ainscow, Hargreaves and Hopkins (1995).)

The six techniques in the series cluster around two key elements in the change process: the individual teacher and the school as an institution. Despite the proliferation of externally mandated changes, the success of many change initiatives remains attributable to the commitment of individual teachers. Certainly the impact of any change on student outcomes is heavily affected by behaviour in the classroom. At the same time, it is claimed that the school as a whole, especially its climate/ethos/culture, makes an important contribution to development and change. Three of the techniques focus on the *individual teacher* and tap data at that level. The other three focus on the *school as an institution*. Data from both levels are essential if the interaction between individual and institution in processes of change is to be better understood. The manual of techniques is accordingly divided into two series.

Series 1: Individual (teacher) level
- *Technique 1: The time line of change* The aim of this technique is to record how individuals within a school perceive their experience of a particular change over a period of time.
- *Technique 2: The experience of change* The purpose of this technique is to gather information about the feelings of individuals towards changes in their school.
- *Technique 3: The initiation of change* This technique taps teachers' commitment to change and their sense of control over it. It differs from the previous two techniques in that it is concerned with change in general rather than a specific change.

Series 2: Institutional (school) level
- *Technique 4: The culture of the school* The purpose of this technique is to generate data on teachers' perceptions of the culture of their school, the direction in which the culture is moving and their ideal culture (see Hargreaves 1995).
- *Technique 5: The structures of the school* The purpose of this technique is to generate data on some of the basic social structures underlying school cultures.
- *Technique 6: The conditions of school* This technique consists of a scale for measuring a school's internal conditions and potential for innovation. The 24 items are grouped under six headings that represent the key conditions necessary for school improvement.

There are a number of ways in which teacher-researchers can use the data generated by the techniques, and feed the data back to schools.

First, because the techniques are amenable to rapid analysis and presentation, virtually immediate feedback can be given in some cases. This is especially true of the culture game, school structures and responses to change techniques. When used with teachers as part of a training day or staff meeting, it is possible to give aggregate responses to the whole staff during the same session. This feedback has often aroused great interest and animated discussion.

The second method of feedback is to talk through the results from the administration of the whole battery with the senior staff of the school involved. There is a method for reducing the data onto one side of A4, and this makes the conveying of information much easier to handle. Our approach is to present the data in a sequential and descriptive way, and then on the basis of this to encourage discussion and interpretation of the results from the senior staff. This proved at times to be a delicate process. Occasionally our ethic of confidentiality is challenged particularly when we are encouraged to be judgemental rather than descriptive. In these discussions it is vital to maintain confidentiality and to not go beyond the data.

The third approach to giving feedback is where the data are used as part of a school improvement process within a school. The techniques are now routinely used in IQEA schools as a basis for action planning. The experience we have had convinces us that the data emerging from the techniques have great heuristic power.

To summarize, when taken together the techniques provide a map of the process of change in a school. They can be used individually to investigate particular aspects of change processes or in combination for a more comprehensive analysis. The techniques can also be used to map changes in the school's conditions over time, and facilitate the process of change and improvement in schools.

In this chapter, I have described a variety of ways in which data can be gathered for the purpose of classroom research. The techniques described in this chapter are basically open-ended insofar as they are used most effectively for diagnostic purposes. Although I have described these techniques individually, it is important to realize that they can and are most often used eclectically and in combination. But each has a specific purpose and is best suited to a particular situation. A taxonomy of the main advantages, disadvantages and uses of the various techniques is given in Table 8.1.

FURTHER READING

Additional information about the techniques of classroom research can be found in the publications associated with the Ford Teaching Project. Elliott and Adelman's (1976) case study of the Ford Teaching Project in the Open University curriculum course *Innovation at the Classroom Level* is informative and useful, as is the Ford Teaching Project booklet *Ways of Doing Research in One's Own Classroom* (Bowen *et al.* n.d.). Walker and Adelman's (1990)

Table 8.1 Taxonomy of classroom research techniques

Technique	Advantage(s)	Disadvantage(s)	Use(s)
Field notes	simple; on-going; personal; aide-mémoire	subjective; needs practice	• specific issue • case study • general impression
Audiotape recording	versatile; accurate; provides ample data	transcription difficult; time-consuming; often inhibiting	• detailed evidence • diagnostic
Pupil diaries	provides pupils' perspective	subjective	• diagnostic • triangulation
Interviews and discussions	can be teacher–pupil, observer–pupil, pupil–pupil	time-consuming	• specific in-depth information
Videotape recorder and digital photography	visual and comprehensive	awkward and expensive; can be distracting	• visual and diagnostic • illustrates critical incidents
Questionnaires	highly specific; easy to administer; comparative	time-consuming to analyse; problem of 'right' answers	• specific information and feedback
Sociometry	easy to administer; provides guide to action	can threaten isolated pupils	• analyses social relationships
Documentary evidence	illuminative	difficult to obtain; time-consuming	• provides context and information
Case study	accurate; representative; uses range of techniques	time-consuming	• comprehensive overview of an issue • publishable format
Mapping techniques	comprehensive; easy to administer and analyse	requires whole staff response; can be threatening; confidentiality sometimes challenged	• provides a map of the process of change in a school • can be used to promote development

book *A Guide to Classroom Observation* is similarly helpful and contains advice on, and examples of, the use of photography in classroom research. Rob Walker's (1989) book *Doing Research* contains detailed advice about methods, as does James McKernan's (1996) *Curriculum Action Research*. Colin Hook's (1981) *Studying Classrooms* is extensive and practical and also contains a useful taxonomy of approaches similar to Table 8.1. Kemmis and McTaggart's (1988) third edition of *The Action Research Planner*, John Elliott's (1991) *Action Research for Educational Change*, John Beresford's (1998) *Collecting Information for School Improvement* and my *Evaluation for School Development* (Hopkins 1989) also contain helpful advice on data collection methods.

CHAPTER 9

Analysing and reporting classroom research data

The third criterion for teacher research outlined in Chapter 4 was that the methodology employed must be reliable enough to allow teachers confidently to formulate hypotheses and develop strategies applicable to their classroom situations. This is an area where teacher research in particular, and qualitative research in general, has not been conspicuously successful. Qualitative research procedures (i.e. where the emphasis is on expressing one's data and conclusions in the form of words) seem often to be shrouded in mystery. The findings of such studies are arrived at by usually unannounced procedures and techniques, thus creating methodologies which can be neither fully scrutinized nor usefully emulated. Consequently, it is important to establish a coherent methodology for analysing classroom research data. In this chapter, I first outline the problem in a little more detail, then suggest a framework for analysis and describe the four stages that comprise the process. I conclude the chapter with a discussion on reporting classroom research findings.

THE PROBLEM

Action research, like most practitioner-oriented methodologies, has been widely criticized, but mainly by those who implicitly denigrate the method by criticizing individual research projects that have adopted classroom research techniques. It is illogical – not to say unfair – to judge the quality of a Shakespeare play by observing a performance by amateur actors. And so it is with classroom research.

It is true though that classroom research is often done badly, mainly because of unarticulated procedures for analysis. By way of contrast, the rules for quasi-experimental research have been cogently articulated (Campbell and Stanley 1963) and have a long and distinguished tradition. This tradition is so prevalent that research in education is commonly equated with studies carried out under this paradigm. This should not be surprising, for the rules are simple to apply and are consistent with the ubiquitous psycho-statistical research tradition. It is unfortunate, as we have seen, that this approach is ill-suited to the research needs of the classroom teacher.

In classroom research, the concern is more with cases than samples. This implies a methodology more applicable to understanding a problematic situation than one based on predicting outcomes within the parameters of an existing and tacitly accepted social system. The skills required of classroom researchers are, as Strauss and Corbin (1998) say, 'The ability to step back and critically analyze situations, to recognize and avoid bias, to obtain valid and reliable data, and to think abstractly.'

Unfortunately, as Miles and Huberman (1984: 20) note in their paper 'Drawing valid meaning from qualitative data', there is an Achilles heel here: there are few agreed canons for the analysis of qualitative data, and therefore the truth claims and validity underlying such work are uncertain. They describe the problem like this:

> Despite a growing interest in qualitative studies, we lack a body of clearly defined methods for drawing valid meaning from qualitative data. We need methods that are practical, communicable, and not self deluding: scientific in the positivist's sense of the word, and aimed toward interpretive understanding in the best sense of that term.

What follows is an attempt to rectify this situation, at least with regards to teacher-based classroom research.

A FRAMEWORK FOR ANALYSIS

Making sense of social situations has long been the task of sociologists and it is from their (and anthropologists') methodological canons that much avant-garde work on educational evaluation was drawn (see Hamilton *et al.* 1977). It is this research tradition that provides a framework within which to consider teacher-based classroom research. Classrooms are also complex social situations that require understanding. We need to produce theory that is applicable to classrooms as well as within them.

Two of the classic statements on sociological fieldwork were made by Becker (1958) and Glaser and Strauss (1967). In his paper 'Problems of inference and proof in participant observation', Becker (1958: 653) described four stages in the analysis of fieldwork data:

We can distinguish three distinct stages of analysis conducted in the field itself, and a fourth stage, carried on after completion of the field work. These stages are differentiated, first, by their logical sequence: each succeeding stage depends on some analysis in the preceding stage. They are further differentiated by the fact that different kinds of conclusions are arrived at in each stage and that these conclusions are put to different uses in the continuing research. Finally, they are differentiated by the different criteria that are used to assess evidence and to reach conclusions in each stage. The three stages of field analysis are: the selection and definition of problems, concepts, and indices; the check on the frequency and distribution of phenomena; and the incorporation of individual findings into a model of the organisation under study. The fourth stage of final analysis involves problems of presentation of evidence and proof.

In a similar way, in *The Discovery of Grounded Theory*, Glaser and Strauss (1967: 105) describe the concept of the constant comparative method as a means of analysing sociological data:

> We shall describe in four stages the constant comparative method; 1. comparing incidents applicable to each category, 2. integrating categories and their properties, 3. delimiting the theory, and 4. writing the theory. Although this method of generating theory is a continuously growing process – each stage after a time is transformed into the next – earlier stages do remain in operation simultaneously throughout the analysis and each provides continuous development to its successive stage until the analysis is terminated.

Although Glaser and Strauss's notion of the constant comparative method is a more dynamic concept than Becker's linear sequence of stages, there are basic similarities in their approaches to the analysis of field data. Each envisage the analytical process as having four distinct generic stages: (1) data collection and the initial generation of categories, (2) validation of categories, (3) interpretation of categories and (4) action. These various stages are summarized in Table 9.1 and represent standard practice for the analysis of qualitative field data. My major point is that this same process can be used by teachers to analyse data emerging from their own classroom research efforts.

Jane: An example

As part of the requirements for a course I taught on the 'Analysis of Teaching', Jane made a videotape of herself experimenting with

Table 9.1 Fieldwork methodology

Classroom research	Becker	Glaser and Strauss
• Data collection	• Selection and definition of concepts	• Compare incidents applicable to each category
• Validation	• Frequency and distribution of concepts	• Integrate categories and their phenomena
• Interpretation	• Incorporation of findings into model	• Delimit theory
• Action	• Presentation of evidence and proof	• Write theory

various models of teaching. After reviewing the videotape, Jane felt that among other observations she had been rather abrupt in her questioning technique and had given the pupils little time to formulate responses to her questions. I suggested to Jane that she explore this observation a little further and ascertain whether this was a consistent behaviour or an aberration. She did this by taking a further videotape of her teaching, and by asking a colleague to observe her teaching. Jane also developed a short questionnaire on her questioning technique, which she administered to her pupils and subsequently analysed. As a result of this endeavour, Jane realized that she did in fact interject very quickly after asking a question, and quite often answered her own questions. All well and good, Jane thought, but what does this mean? Thinking that recent research on teaching might help, Jane did some reading and came across an article on think-time. The article reviewed a number of studies on the relationship between the amount of time that elapsed after questioning and the quality of pupil response. Jane felt that she was not allowing her pupils enough time to think after she had asked a question to the detriment perhaps of their level of cognitive functioning. So she developed a plan to change and monitor her questioning technique. It took Jane some six months to complete these tasks (teaching is a time-consuming job!), but there was no pressure on her to complete the research. In fact, the longer time-frame allowed for more valid data, and she was pleased with the results. Not only did she find evidence of higher-level responses from her pupils, but also, by involving them in the evaluation of her teaching, the climate of her class was enhanced by the mutual and overt commitment of both teacher and pupils to the learning process.

DATA COLLECTION

In the classroom research process, the first step is collecting data. With the use of, say, a videotape recorder, or any other of a range of methods, the teacher gathers information about his or her teaching. Having collected the data, a substage follows immediately or co-exists with the collection of data – the generation of hypotheses. We are always generating ideas to explain classroom events. Even at the earliest stages of research, we are interpreting and explaining to ourselves 'why this is happening' and 'what caused that'. It is inevitable that as individuals we bring our experience and beliefs to bear upon situations that we wish to understand better. As Popper says, 'observations . . . are always interpretations of the facts observed . . . they are interpretations in the light of theories' (quoted in Magee 1973: 107). Popper's use of the word theory implies, of course, not only 'grand' theory, but also personal theory – the presuppositions, assumptions and beliefs that guide our actions.

At the end of the data collection stage, not only have we collected our data, but we have also established a number of hypotheses, constructs or categories that begin to explain what is happening in the classroom. These hypotheses (I am using the word broadly) usually emerge quite naturally from the data-gathering process. Jane, in the example, generated a number of ideas about her teaching from viewing the videotape. Among these was an observation that she was too abrupt in her questioning technique and had given her pupils too little time to answer questions. These hypotheses not only reflect the data but are also an interpretation of them. At this stage, the more ideas the better. The richer and more creative our thoughts, the more likely it is that the research will result in a coherent and complete interpretation of the problem. It is in the following stage that we begin to evaluate the hypotheses, so initially one should be as creative and as suggestive as possible.

VALIDATION

The second stage in the process concerns the validation of the hypotheses. I will suggest a number of techniques for establishing the validity of a category or hypothesis. Of all these 'tests for trustworthiness', triangulation is most probably the best known, and so I describe it first.

The technique of *triangulation* was popularized by John Elliott and Clem Adelman during their work with the Ford Teaching Project. It involves contrasting the perceptions of one actor in a specific situation against those of other actors in the same situation. By doing this, an initial subjective observation or perception is fleshed out and given a degree of authenticity. Elliott and Adelman (1976: 74) describe the technique thus:

Triangulation involves gathering accounts of a teaching situation from three quite different points of view; namely those of the teacher, his pupils, and a participant observer. Who in the 'triangle' gathers the accounts, how they are elicited, and who compares them, depends largely on the context. The process of gathering accounts from three distinct standpoints has an epistemological justification. Each point of the triangle stands in a unique epistemological position with respect to access to relevant data about a teaching situation. The teacher is in the best position to gain access via introspection to his own intentions and aims in the situation. The students are in the best position to explain how the teacher's actions influence the way they respond in the situation. The participant observer is in the best position to collect data about the observable features of the interaction between teachers and pupils. By comparing his own account with accounts from the other two standpoints a person at one point of the triangle has an opportunity to test and perhaps revise it on the basis of more sufficient data.

Jane, in the example, validated her observations through triangulation. She had another teacher observe her teaching and she also gave her pupils a questionnaire on her questioning technique. From this evidence, she was able to validate and refine the observation from three different sources.

It must be admitted that triangulation is not always an easy process to engage in. Initially, it may be threatening for a teacher to involve students in the evaluation of their teaching, or it may prove difficult to obtain the services of a peer to act as a participant observer. Teachers with the personal openness and interest in their teaching needed to initiate such research will, however, eventually overcome these difficulties. Incidentally, I believe that it is important for the teacher to involve his or her pupils in the research process as soon as their confidence allows. Young people provide wonderfully frank and honest feedback, especially when they sense that their opinions are valued and respected, and this can only serve to enhance the quality of life in the classroom. The teacher must, however, be careful to introduce this change in his or her teaching slowly and self-consciously, being fully aware that pupils are a potentially conservative force within the classroom and often need to be 'broken in' to new ideas and different styles (Rudduck 1984).

Another well-known technique is *saturation*. Becker (1958) and Glaser and Strauss (1967) point to a similar process: Becker refers to 'the check on the frequency and distribution of phenomenon' (p. 653) and Glaser and Strauss to 'saturation', a situation where 'no additional data are being found ... [to] develop properties of the category' (p. 67). When applied to the classroom research situation, this implies that the hypothesis or category generated from observation is tested repeatedly against the data in an attempt to modify or falsify it.

It is difficult and perhaps reckless to suggest a frequency that ensures the validity of a category, for that will vary from case to case, but during this process a number of predictable events can occur. First, if on repeated testing the category is found wanting it is then discarded. Second, the category may have been conceptualized crudely and, through testing, the concept is modified, refined and amplified. Third, although the process of falsification (in the Popperian sense) is never complete, there comes a time when repeated observation leads neither to refutation nor amplification and only serves to support the hypothesis. At this point, when the utility of observation decreases, saturation can be said to have occurred and the hypothesis has been validated.

Referring to the example of Jane, having decided to explore her questioning technique further, she videotaped herself again and found that, in fact, she was quite abrupt in her questioning and interjected far too quickly. In this way, she firmly validated the observation by saturating it.

There are a number of other techniques for establishing validity which I will describe more briefly. But before I do, I should distinguish between *validity*, which reflects the internal consistency of one's research, and *reliability*, which reflects the generalizability of one's findings. In general, most classroom researchers and those who use qualitative methods are concerned with validity rather than reliability; insofar as their focus is a particular case rather than a sample.

In the same way as one triangulates the perception of various individuals, so too must we triangulate our *sources of data*. There are, as we have seen, many data sources open to the classroom researcher, e.g. surveys, questionnaires, observation, interviews and documents. The matrix shown later in Figure 9.1 helps illustrate the range of data sources available at different levels of analysis. Although not every cell should be completed, a wide scatter should usually be employed. Each data source gives information of a different type which usually serves to complement and provide a check on the others.

Two other common techniques used at this stage of analysis are *rival explanations* and the search for *negative cases*. Michael Patton (1990: 327–8) describes these techniques like this:

> When considering rival hypotheses and competing explanations the strategy to be employed is not one of attempting to disprove the alternatives; rather, the analyst looks for data that *support* alternative explanations. Failure to find strong supporting evidence for alternative explanations helps increase confidence in the original, principal explanation.

Closely related to the testing of alternative explanations is the search for negative cases. Where patterns and trends have been identified, our understanding of those patterns and trends is increased by considering the instances and cases that do not fit within the pattern.

I use the phrase *call things by their right name* to describe the next technique, which is nicely illustrated by Humpty Dumpty when he said: 'When I use a word it means just what I choose it to mean – neither more or less.' The point is an obvious one – we need to know what we are looking for. As classroom researchers, we have to do our conceptual work properly. We should be aware, for example, of suggesting that a child who is looking intently at a teacher is in fact paying attention; or of dictionary definitions that define intelligence as mental ability; or of operational definitions that regard paying attention as not looking out of the window. None of these help us very much. Conceptualization involves articulating a full, clear and coherent account of what constitutes being an instance of something; that is to say, it necessitates elaborating the criteria that have to be met if, for example, a pupil is legitimately to be described as engaging in enquiry/discovery learning (Barrow 1986). This may be difficult to do at the outset, but the clarification of concepts should always be a major concern throughout the research process.

An *audit trail* is a technique used to increase the validity of one's data and which borrows its name from the concept of a financial audit. Schwandt and Halpern (1988: 73) describe the usefulness of an audit trail, or of establishing a chain of evidence, in this way:

> Preparing an audit trail is important for two reasons. First, it documents the inquiry in a fashion that facilitates a third-party examination. The audit trail contains information that describes the methods used to control error and to reach justifiable conclusions . . . Second, an audit trail helps [classroom researchers] manage their record keeping. They find an organized trail useful when they need to retrieve information easily and when they prepare their final reports . . . [it helps them] become more thoughtful, critical, and reflective.

Another widely used strategy for ensuring validity is having *key respondents* review drafts of one's research reports. This can either be the people involved in the research (one's colleagues or students), or those knowledgeable about the situation you are enquiring into. To the extent that those involved in the research do not recognize the description and analysis in the report, then its validity is suspect. Involving others in the research is also a worthwhile activity in itself.

Let me now restate the important methodological point. I am arguing that by employing analytical techniques such as triangulation and the other methods just described, teacher-researchers can produce hypotheses and concepts that are valid, methodologically sound and to an extent generalizable.

By engaging in this process of hypothesis generation, teacher-researchers are producing what Glaser and Strauss have called grounded theory, because it is theory grounded in data gathered from and applicable to a specific social situation. By utilizing this methodology, we can have confidence in our subsequent actions for, as Dunn and Swierczek (1977: 137) comment:

> The application of grounded theories promises to contribute to improvements in the degree to which findings
>
> 1 reflect conditions actually present in particular change efforts (internal validity);
> 2 typify conditions actually present in other change efforts (external validity);
> 3 contribute to the generation of new concepts by constantly comparing information obtained by different methods (reflexivity); and
> 4 promote understanding among groups with conflicting frames of reference.

INTERPRETATION

The third stage in the research process is interpretation. This involves taking a validated hypothesis and fitting it into a frame of reference that gives it meaning. For the classroom researcher, this means taking a hypothesis and relating it either to theory, the norms of accepted practice or the teacher's own intuition as to what comprises good teaching. This allows the teacher-researcher to give meaning to a particular observation or series of observations that can lead profitably to action. In doing this, the classroom researcher is creating meaning out of hitherto discrete observations and constructs.

Jane gave meaning to her hypothesis by reading about 'think-time'. That information not only helped her understand the implications of her behaviour but also suggested a direction for action.

ACTION

The final step in the process is action. Having created meaning out of the research data, the teacher-researcher is in a position to plan for future action. Building on the evidence gathered during the research, the teacher is able to plan realistic strategies which are themselves monitored by class-room research procedures. Jane did just that. The interpretation stage gave her information on how to change her questioning technique, which after some planning she attempted to monitor and evaluate.

THE ON-GOING PROCESS OF DATA ANALYSIS

The analysis of data is a very important part of the classroom research process. It is only at this stage that the teacher can be certain that the results obtained are valid and trustworthy. When teacher-researchers fail to analyse their data adequately, they lack a secure platform for action. The four stages of classroom research are outlined in Box 9.1.

   The four stages of classroom research, although based on sociological research methods, are, in fact, only organized common sense. These stages are also far more interactive than the linear description given so far in this chapter would imply. In fact, the whole process is in reality a very dynamic one. There are two aspects of this 'dynamism' that I want to mention in particular.

   In Figure 9.1, there is a matrix that illustrates the range of data sources available at each stage of analysis. As noted earlier, not every cell of the matrix needs to be completed. The point to be made here is that in the initial phase, one analyses the questionnaire or interview schedules, then uses the analysed data from a number of different sources to generate the categories or hypotheses. Having done that, one validates them in the second phase and then returns to phase one to collect more data. This on-going process of data collection and verification is a characteristic of the analysis of qualitative or naturalistic research data.

   The second point is that the *whole* process is interactive. Matthew Miles and Michael Huberman, whose concern about the lack of agreement on methods for analysis we have already noted, have written a very practical and detailed book called *Qualitative Data Analysis*. In it they describe

Box 9.1   Four stages of classroom research

---

   1 *Data collection* and the generation of categories or hypotheses.

   2 *Validation* of categories or hypotheses using the techniques for trustworthiness, such as triangulation.

   3 *Interpretation* by reference to theory, agreed criteria, established practice or teacher judgement.

   4 *Action* for development that is also monitored by classroom research techniques.

Analysis	Information source				
	Surveys	Questionnaires	Observations	Interviews	Documents
1 Data collection and the generation of categories or hypotheses					
2 Validation of categories or hypotheses					
3 Interpretation by reference to theory, agreed criteria, established practice or teacher judgement					
4 Plan action for development					

Figure 9.1 A matrix for analysing classroom research data.

the interactive model of data analysis like this (Miles and Huberman 1994: 21–2):

> *Data reduction*: Data reduction refers to the process of selecting, focusing, simplifying, abstracting and transforming the 'raw' data that appear in written up field notes. As data collection proceeds, there are further episodes of data reduction (doing summaries, coding, teasing out themes, making clusters, making partitions, writing memos). And the data reduction/transforming process continues after fieldwork, until a final report is complete.
>
> *Data display*: The second major flow of analysis activity is data display. We define a 'display' as an organised assembly of information that permits conclusion drawing and action taking. Looking at displays helps us to understand what is happening and to do something – further analysis or action – based on that understanding.
>
> *Conclusion drawing/verification*: The third stream of analysis activity is conclusion drawing and verification. From the beginning of data collection, the [classroom researcher] is beginning to decide what things mean, is noting regularities, patterns, explanations, possible configurations, causal flows and propositions. The competent researcher holds these conclusions lightly, maintaining openness and scepticism, but the conclusions are still there, inchoate and vague at first, then increasingly explicit and grounded.

In this sense, qualitative data analysis is a continuous, iterative enterprise. Issues of data reduction of display, and of conclusion drawing/verification come into figure successfully as analysis episodes follow each other.

REPORTING RESEARCH

The link between research and action has been an implicit theme through-out this book. To teacher-researchers, research alone is a necessary but not sufficient condition: research has to feed action and development. The class-room research process described in previous chapters has as its goal profes-sional development and the enhancement of classroom performance. The fourth stage in the analytical framework discussed in this chapter is action, which itself is monitored and researched using classroom research procedures. This is the crowning achievement of the research process. In this concluding section, I want to look at some of the ways in which the action and information, generated by the research process, can be reported.

There are a number of different ways of reporting teacher research efforts. I have seen them range from loose anecdotal accounts to highly 'scientific' and formal research reports submitted for a higher degree. In many instances, teachers who engage in classroom research have no need to present their results to anyone except to themselves, particularly if the research is to be used solely to enhance their teaching. Despite this, I think that all teacher-researchers need to put their data together in such a way that:

- The research could be replicated on another occasion.
- The evidence used to generate hypotheses and consequent action is clearly documented.
- Action taken as a result of the research is monitored.
- The reader finds the research accessible and that it resonates with his or her own experience.

This process of setting a clear purpose, of using a methodology which provides valid results, and then using these as a basis for action, can be made relatively straightforward if the researcher keeps a loose-leaf log or diary as the research progresses. An on-going research diary like this also provides an invaluable basis for reflection and is great fun to look at with the wisdom of hindsight. It provides an excellent record of how one's views and attitudes evolve over time.

If one does want or need to prepare a research report, there are many ways of doing this. To begin with, there is the rather traditional approach that uses as a guide, points similar to the following:

1 *Statement of intent*
   - clarify purpose,
   - rationale.
2 *Procedures and process*
   - research design,
   - techniques of data collection,

- verification of concepts,
- what actually occurred.

3 *Results and implementation*
   - outcomes of research,
   - theoretical implications,
   - action taken as a result,
   - evaluation of action.

4 *Meta-analysis*
   - review whole process,
   - conclusions as to the usefulness of the research,
   - what would you do differently next time.

The purpose of this outline is to provide teacher researchers with a framework for their report. While this is important, what perhaps is even more critical is that the format of a report encourages the teacher to stand back and to examine the process systematically by making a meta-analysis of the research.

Classroom researchers should not feel constrained by the traditional research report format when sharing the product of their research. There are any number of formats that can be used. As long as the procedures outlined in previous chapters are followed, then imagination is the only limit on the possibilities of presentation. Here are a few examples:

- *Cartoons*: often classroom researchers use the cartoon format to get a key finding from their research across in a powerful and accessible way.
- *Video*: a visual representation using video or digital camera provides concrete images that an audience can relate to their own situation.
- *Fiction*: using data or constructs from the research to tell a story often encourages reflection and discussion more effectively than the traditional report. As long as the quotations or events are 'real', then a fictional setting may enhance the message.
- *Data reduction and display*: displaying reduced data is often a powerful way of stimulating discussion. This approach allows large amounts of data to be displayed economically and it could be accompanied by another page of questions, commentary or explanation that highlighted the main issues.

Classroom researchers should not be afraid to experiment with different ways of presenting their work, as long as the information is valid and has been carefully analysed. The fundamental point is that action should result from the research.

Let us assume that a classroom researcher has generated some valid 'knowledge'. What key conditions must be present if someone is to take action congruent with the knowledge? Here, Louis and Miles (1992: 289) take a cut at what might be required:

- *Clarity*: The knowledge must be understood clearly – not be fuzzy, vague or confusing.
- *Relevance*: The knowledge is seen as meaningful, as connected to one's normal life and concerns – not irrelevant, inapplicable, impractical.
- *Action images*: The knowledge is or can become exemplified in specific actions, clearly visualized. Without such images, knowledge-based action is unlikely.
- *Will*: There must be motivation, interest, action orientation, and a will to do something with the knowledge.
- *Skill*: There must be actual behavioural ability to do the action envisioned. Without skill, the action will either be aborted or done incongruently with the knowledge undergirding it.

Colin Hook (1981: 291–2), in his book *Studying Classrooms*, provides a helpful checklist of questions that can be used to review one's research report or any other format for presenting classroom research:

- Did I collect the information as planned? Did it provide the information I needed?
- What problems did I have? What could I have done better? Should I employ other data-gathering methods?
- Did I gather all relevant available information? Should I have gathered pupils' opinions, parental views, and other teachers' feelings?
- In what ways can I use the information to make more effective teacher decisions? Is further information required?
- Can the information obtained be interpreted in other ways? Are my interpretations and conclusions valid?
- Have I presented the information in a clear way? Does the information indicate future teaching actions?
- Can I discuss the information with pupils, colleagues or parents?
- Who else could have been involved, how and when?
- What did I, the pupils, parents, colleagues, etc., get out of the investigation?
- What changes should I make in future investigations? Do my pupils, colleagues, etc., have suggestions?
- Can I interest colleagues in co-ordinating action research approaches, to collaborate in future studies?
- Do other teachers share my concerns? Do other teachers have skills which may help me in self-monitoring?

The dynamics of the analysis stage adds to the complexity of what is already the most difficult part of the classroom research process. The procedures described in this chapter, however, make good working guidelines in any form of qualitative enquiry, be it to inform the thought processes of a group of teachers sitting together for an hour to discuss their classroom research, or researchers involved in an international multi-site case study. Qualitative research is less of a methodology and more a way of life! It is an approach that is applicable across a range of settings, describes and analyses phenomena on their own terms, and helps us to think constructively and to generate meaning out of complex and problematic situations. Consequently, it is also an approach that empowers individuals and increases feelings of efficacy. This sense of efficacy can only develop if we share and report our methodological procedures and establish a genuinely collaborative and critical research community that is committed to informed action.

FURTHER READING

This is complex territory which I have tried to present as simply as I can in this chapter. More detailed accounts can be found in my *Evaluation for School Development* (Hopkins 1989: Ch.5) and a more detailed paper (Hopkins *et al.* 1989). Since the mid-1970s, there has been a growing interest in illuminative, anthropological and ethnographic research approaches. Much of this literature is technical and not ideally suited for our purposes. However, the book by Hammersley and Atkinson (1995), *Ethnography: Principles in Practice*, provides an excellent overview of the field and an introduction to the literature. Lincoln and Guba's (1985) *Naturalistic Inquiry* is also a useful source, as is Patton's (1990) *Qualitative Evaluation Methods. Beyond the Numbers Game* (Hamilton *et al.* 1977) is a comprehensive statement on the illuminative (or new wave) tradition in educational evaluation and research, mainly from the UK perspective. One of the most helpful sections in this collection is the discussion of alternative methodology, especially the work of Louis Smith. Clem Adelman's book, *Uttering, Muttering* (1981), on linguistic research in classrooms contains an helpful chapter on triangulation. McCormick and James's (1989) book on *Curriculum Evaluation in Schools*, besides being an excellent general source, contains some very helpful sections on validity and reliability.

The references mentioned in the text should also be consulted, especially Becker (1958) and Glaser and Strauss (1967), although the latter may prove to be a little hard going. Fortunately, two books by Strauss (1987) and Strauss and Corbin (1998) prove more accessible. The first chapter of Strauss's *Qualitative Analysis for Social Scientists* provides an exemplary introduction to grounded theory. Anyone seriously interested in educational research should also be familiar with Campbell and Stanley's (1963) classic 'Experimental and quasi-experimental designs for research on teaching'. Although written from a different perspective from this book, its discussion of research designs and the concepts of internal and external validity are essential knowledge for those involved in educational research. It should be noted that Miles and Huberman's (1994) *Qualitative Data Analysis* is the essential source book for anyone interested in the ideas and themes touched on in this chapter. Finally, the discussion of reporting research and publication was quite extensive and the main sources were cited. In addition, the various collections of case studies referred to elsewhere in the book provide examples of different ways and styles of reporting. The texts by Rob Walker (*Doing Research*, 1989), Judith Bell (*Doing Your Research Project*, third edition, 1999), Jean McNiff (*Action Research*, 1992) and Colin Hook (*Studying Classrooms*, 1981) provide further advice.

CHAPTER 10

Teaching and learning as the heartland of classroom research

Despite the contemporary emphasis on the importance of classroom practice, the language of discourse about teaching remains in general at a restricted level. There is a need for a far more elaborate language in which to talk about teaching and more sophisticated frameworks against which to reflect on practice. Even in those instances where more precision of language is achieved, say in the debate on whole class teaching, there are few operational definitions against which teachers can assess their own practice and thereby develop and expand their range of classroom practices. Quality teaching and learning needs to be underpinned by more elaborate and explicit frameworks for learning and teaching.

In this chapter, I discuss some of the evidence on effective teaching and learning. This is for two reasons. The first is in order to provide a sharper focus for classroom research activities that relate to teaching and learning. The second is to offer specifications that can contribute to broader and richer discourse about the nature of teaching and learning.

Although the evidence on effective teaching can help teachers become more creative in creating powerful learning environments for students, such research and strategies, however, should not be regarded as panaceas to be followed slavishly. Research knowledge and the various specifications of teaching can have many limitations, especially if they are adopted uncritically. Such knowledge only becomes useful when it is subjected to the discipline of practice through the exercise of the teacher's professional judgement. For, as Lawrence Stenhouse (1975: 142) said, such proposals are not to be regarded 'as an unqualified recommendation, but rather as a provisional specification claiming no more than to be worth putting to the test of practice. Such proposals claim to be intelligent rather than correct.'

As has been seen throughout this book, outstanding teachers take individual and collective responsibility to base their teaching on the best knowledge and practice available. But they then take those ideas and strategies and critically reflect on them through practice in their own and each other's classrooms. It is through reflection that the teacher harmonizes, integrates and transcends the necessary classroom management skills, the acquisition of a repertoire of models of teaching, and the personal aspects of his or her teaching into a strategy that has meaning for the students. This is the heartland of the synergy between teaching and learning and classroom research.

In developing the theme of this chapter I:

- discuss the nature of powerful learning;
- describe some of the evidence related to effective teaching;
- outline the concept of a model of teaching;
- provide examples of three common teaching models; and,
- reflect on the nature of teaching style.

POWERFUL LEARNING

There is now an increasingly sophisticated literature on how learning occurs and on the ways in which the learning experience can be organized to make a positive difference to students. The impact is not just on test scores and examination results, but also on the students' learning capability. This is the heart of the matter. If the teacher can teach the student how to learn at the same time as assisting them to acquire curriculum content then the twin goals of learning and achievement can be met.

The purpose of teaching therefore is not only to help students to acquire curriculum knowledge but also to assist them in becoming powerful learners. The most effective curricular and teaching patterns induce students to construct knowledge – to inquire into subject areas intensively. The result is to increase student capacity to learn and work smarter. The trick of course is to find ways of raising levels of attainment whilst at the same time helping students become more powerful learners by expanding and making articulate their repertoire of learning strategies.

Powerful learning refers to the ability of learners to respond successfully to the tasks that they are set, as well as the tasks they set themselves – in particular to:

- integrate prior and new knowledge,
- acquire and use a range of learning skills,
- solve problems individually and in groups,

- think carefully about their successes and failures,
- evaluate conflicting evidence and to think critically,
- accept that learning involves uncertainty and difficulty.

The deployment of such a range of learning strategies is commonly termed meta-cognition, which can be regarded as the learner's ability to take control over their own learning processes. The key point is that within whatever context learning takes place, it involves an 'active construction of meaning'. This carries implications for the management of learning opportunities. As learning is interactional, it occurs only when the learner makes sense of particular experiences in particular contexts. This 'making sense' involves connecting with an individual's prior knowledge and experience. Thus, new learning has to relate to, and ultimately 'fit with', what individuals already understand. Learning should therefore be seen as a process as much as producing end results.

The central characteristic of effective teachers therefore is their ability to create powerful learners as well as knowledgeable students. The purpose of the framework for teaching proposed below, is to help all teachers to do just that.

EFFECTIVE TEACHING

There is an extensive research literature on effective teaching. Consistently high correlations are achieved between student achievement scores and the teacher's classroom behaviour (see Brophy and Good 1986; Creemers 1994). One general conclusion stands out: 'The most consistently replicated findings link achievement to the quantity and pacing of instruction' (Brophy and Good 1986: 360). The amount learned is as Good (1989) subsequently noted, determined in part by opportunity to learn, which is determined by four broad teacher behaviours:

- First, the extent to which teachers are businesslike and task-oriented, emphasise instruction as basic to their role, expect students to master the curriculum, and allocate most classroom time to those activities that have relevant academic objectives.
- Second, teachers whose students make reasonable academic progress frequently use classroom organization and management strategies that maximize the time students spend engaged in academic activities.
- Third, effective teachers allow students to move through the curriculum briskly but also relatively successfully.

- Fourth, these teachers were found to spend most of their time actively instructing their students in group lessons or supervising their work on assignments rather than allowing students to spend inordinate time on individual seatwork practice without supervision or feedback.

Classroom studies of teaching effects have generally supported a direct and structured approach to instruction (Doyle 1987: 96); that is, students usually achieve more when a teacher:

- Emphasizes academic goals, makes them explicit, and expects students to be able to master the curriculum;
- Carefully organises and sequences curriculum experiences;
- Clearly explains and illustrates what students are to learn;
- Frequently asks direct and specific questions to monitor students' progress and check their understanding;
- Provides students with ample opportunity to practise, gives prompts and feedback to ensure success, corrects mistakes, and allows students to use a skill until it is over-learned or automatic;
- Reviews regularly and holds students accountable for work.

From this perspective, a teacher promotes student learning by being active in planning and organizing his or her teaching, explaining to students what they are to learn, arranging occasions for guided practice, monitoring progress, providing feedback, and otherwise helping students understand and accomplish work.

At the heart of the teacher's work, of course, is classroom management. If classrooms are to be places where students can feel safe to concentrate on the tasks they are set, teachers have to be skilled in organizing and managing large groups of people within a relatively confined space. Evertson and Harris (1992: 76) for example, have identified the following highlights of research on classroom management:

- Use time as effectively as possible;
- Implement group strategies with high levels of involvement and low levels of misbehaviour;
- Choose lesson formats and academic tasks conducive to high student engagement;
- Communicate clearly rules of participation;
- Prevent problems by implementing a system at the beginning of the school year.

During our school improvement work we find it helpful to encourage teachers to look at some of the specific issues involved and the skills that are required. In this context we use short summaries of research evidence to stimulate discussion between groups of colleagues. For example, Kounin (1970) in his classic study identified several strategies that teachers use to elicit high levels of work involvement and low levels of misbehaviour:

- *Withitness* – communicating awareness of student behaviour;
- *Overlapping* – doing more than one thing at once;
- *Smoothness and momentum* – moving in and out of activities smoothly with appropriately paced and sequenced instruction; and
- *Group alerting* – keeping all students attentive to a whole group focus.

MODELS OF TEACHING

Despite the impressive gains associated in the research literature with the range of teaching skills described above, they should be regarded as a necessary but not sufficient condition for effective teaching. There is a further and equally strong body of research and practice that suggests that student achievement can be further enhanced by the consistent and strategic use of specific teaching models (Joyce and Weil 1996; Joyce *et al.* 1997). There are many powerful models of teaching – each with their own 'syntax', phases and guidelines – that are designed to bring about particular kinds of learning and to help students become more effective learners.

As was implied earlier, models of teaching are really models of learning. As students acquire information, ideas, skills, values, ways of thinking, and means of expressing themselves, they are also learning how to learn. In fact, the most important long-term outcome of teaching may be the students' increased capabilities to learn more easily and effectively in the future, both because of the knowledge and skill they have acquired, and because they have mastered learning processes. How teaching is conducted has a large impact on students' abilities to educate themselves (Joyce *et al.* 1997: 15).

It is important to be clear about what is meant by a 'model of teaching'. One can regard the research on teaching effects or teaching skills as providing the teacher with say tactical knowledge. The research on 'models of teaching' on the other hand gives teachers more strategic knowledge, about how to create whole classroom settings to facilitate learning.

A well known, if dated, example of a model of teaching related to the theme of this book is that of the Humanities Curriculum Project (HCP). As was mentioned in Chapter 1, the HCP was developed under the aegis of the Schools Council in England by a team led by Lawrence Stenhouse (1970, 1975, 1983). In this curriculum, discussion was the main mode of enquiry and the teacher acted as a neutral chairperson. Discussion was informed and disciplined by evidence, such as items from history, journalism and literature. This particular curriculum approach inevitably placed new kinds of demand on both teachers and pupils (Rudduck 1984: 57). For example:

> *New skills for most teachers:*
> - Discussion rather than instruction;
> - Teacher as neutral chairperson;
> - Teacher talk reduced to about 15 per cent of the total talking done in the classroom;
> - Teacher handling material from different disciplines;
> - New modes of assessment.
>
> *New skills for most pupils:*
> - Discussion, not argument or debate;
> - Listening to, and talking to, each other, not just the teacher;
> - Taking initiatives in contributing – not being cued by the teacher.

There is a danger that centrally designed curricula can become blueprints that inhibit autonomy in teaching and learning. In that respect it is interesting to note that the Humanities Curriculum as a model of teaching was specific rather than prescriptive. Although it defined the educational encounter, it also encouraged teachers to experiment with the specificity rather than be bound by the prescription. From this perspective, the process model of curriculum, as described by Stenhouse (1975), is liberating or emancipatory because it encourages independence of thought and argument on the part of the pupil, and experimentation and the use of judgement on the part of the teacher. When teachers adopt this experimental approach to their teaching they are taking on an educational idea, cast in the form of a curriculum proposal and testing it out within their classrooms. It is in this way that the use of 'teaching models' form part of an overall strategy for school improvement.

In *Models of Learning – Tools for Teaching* (Joyce *et al.* 1997) and the *Creating Conditions for Teaching and Learning* (Hopkins and Harris 2000) handbook based on experiences in IQEA schools, a range of contrasting and complementary teaching strategies are described. These are drawn from Joyce's original four families of teaching models, namely the information processing, the social, the personal, and the behavioural families (Joyce and Weil 1996).

These models of teaching (actually models for learning) simultaneously define the nature of the content, the learning strategies, and the arrangements for social interaction that create the learning environments of students. All of the models are research-based insofar as they have been developed and refined through cycles of development and evaluation and have proven effectiveness.

Table 10.1 Relationship between model of teaching and learning skills

Model of teaching	Learning skill
Advanced organizer (or whole class teaching model)	Extracting information and ideas from lectures and presentations
Group work	Working effectively with others to initiate and carry out cooperative tasks
Inductive teaching	Building hypotheses and theories through classification

Models of teaching are also models of learning. How teaching is conducted has a large impact on students' abilities to educate themselves. So for example, if in whole class teaching the teacher uses the advance organizer model to structure a presentation, the student can use the same method as a means of extracting information and ideas from lectures and presentations. The relationship between the model of teaching and of learning of three of the most commonly used models in IQEA schools is seen in Table 10.1.

When these models and strategies are combined, they have even greater potential for improving student learning. Thus imagine a classroom where the learning environment contains a variety of models of teaching that are not only intended to accomplish a range of curriculum goals, but are also designed to help students increase their competence as learners.

In such classrooms the students learn models for memorizing information, how to attain concepts and how to invent them. They practise building hypotheses and theories and using the tools of science to test them. They learn how to extract information and ideas from lectures and presentations, how to study social issues and how to analyse their own social values. These students also know how to profit from training and how to train themselves in athletics, performing arts, mathematics and social skills. They know how to make their writing and problem solving more lucid and creative. Perhaps most importantly, they know how to take initiative in planning personal study, and they know how to work with others to initiate and carry out cooperative tasks. As students master information and skills, the result of each learning experience is not only the content they learn but also the greater ability they acquire to approach future learning tasks with confidence and to create increasingly effective learning environments for themselves.

The models of teaching are therefore simply tools that teachers can use to create more powerful learning experiences. In the following sections examples are given of the models of teaching and learning identified in Table 10.1.

THE WHOLE CLASS TEACHING MODEL

In active whole class teaching the teacher controls pupils' learning and seeks to improve performance through direct instruction, whole class questioning, discussion and learning activities (adapted from Hopkins and Harris 2000).

> A class of Year 7 pupils is being introduced to rhythm in poetry as part of a unit on sound effects in language. The objectives of the lesson are to refine pupils' listening powers in particular their sense of volume, beat and pace; to appreciate the force of repetition and variation of tempo; to understand the relationship between meaning and beat; to appreciate how writers use these elements to create dramatic effects in their writing. The teacher has chosen Vachel Lindsay's ballad, *The Daniel Jazz*, as an example.
>
> The lesson begins with the title of the poem. The class is asked to work out what it means. Who was Daniel? What has jazz got to do with him? There is a whole class discussion to ascertain prior knowledge of the class using a range of questioning techniques. Taking the medley of ideas, the teacher builds up a complete version of the story for the class.
>
> The teacher then develops the jazz/story connection and challenges the class to say what they understand by 'jazz writing'. Students are asked to write down at least two ideas on the relationship between music and words. Students share their ideas with the person next to them and together they produce two or three more ideas.
>
> After a few minutes the teacher asks for responses to the questions and elicits terms which might include: DRUM BEAT, RHYTHM, NOISE, LOUD, FAST, SLOW, BASS, TIMING, REPETITION and so on. Some of these concepts are written on the board and stay as reference points for the rest of the lesson.
>
> The teacher then displays the first ten lines of *The Daniel Jazz*. Teacher reads the first four lines and asks if any of the words on the board apply to this section of the poem. Class recites the lines together emphasizing the beat. A *Sun* newspaper report of the Daniel incident at a local zoo is introduced to the class. The class tries to recite it but fail. The difference between the two pieces of writing is posed as a question to the class.
>
> In pairs, the class is asked to identify any differences in pace and rhythm in the first 20 lines of the poem. After a few minutes pairs report back with examples. At this point the teacher can assess the degree to which the concepts are being understood and adjust teaching accordingly. More demonstration may be needed to re-inforce the concepts of rhythm and pace.

A provided worksheet asks pupils to identify the slow and fast lines in the 20 lines they are now getting familiar with and explain in the writing space provided what makes them slow and why the writer has varied the pace. Partners discuss their results and then the teacher asks for some examples praising and refining pupil contributions as is appropriate.

The conclusion to the lesson is an accretive recital. Two pupils say the first line, then two more join in for the second and so on until the whole class are jazzing their way through the lines, feeling the beat.

This model of teaching enables pupils to order, absorb, understand and relate different areas of knowledge efficiently. It is not a matter of instruction alone. As well as enabling students to process information, the model also allows for pupil interaction so that they learn from each other as well as the teacher and extend their repertoire of social skills. Whole class teaching is about talking with pupils, listening to them and guiding their learning activities.

Whole class active teaching is essentially composed of three components or phases:

1 Pupils are formally presented with a problem, issue, area of knowledge, set of skills through lecture or demonstration.
2 Pupils develop understanding through systematic questioning and disciplined enquiry.
3 Pupils apply understanding through a series of set tasks.

The model pre-supposes a coherent instructional programme based on a clear set of overarching goals. The model though is not inclusive to these goals. The instructional model works as part of an integrative teaching and learning plan that may include cooperative group work and independent study. Employing a range of teaching activities influences pupil motivation and is likely to engage them in learning. Non-stop teacher presentation or instruction involving taking notes, answering questions from textbooks and recycling information in homework is tedious and repetitive. Mixing the palette of teaching approaches is more likely to engage pupils in learning, as will mixing modes of delivery and format.

It is important to emphasize that whole class teaching is a strategic approach to teaching that not only focuses on basic skills and cognitive processes, but also on promoting learning strategies, problem solving and social support. Teachers using the whole class model address these more complex instructional goals by using a range of techniques to structure strategic learning. Some of these key strategies are (adapted from Good and Brophy 1997):

- *Understanding*. This is a prerequisite to clarity and involves matching the new information to the learners' present knowledge. Does the teacher:

  - Determine students' existing familiarity with the information presented?
  - Use terms that are unambiguous and within the students' experience?

- *Structuring*. This involves organizing the material to promote a clear presentation; stating the purpose, reviewing main ideas, and providing transitions between sections. Does the teacher:

  - Establish the purpose of the lesson?
  - Preview the organization of the lesson?
  - Include internal summaries of the lesson?

- *Sequencing*. This involves arranging the information in an order conducive to learning, typically by gradually increasing its difficulty or complexity. Does the teacher:

  - Order the lesson in a logical way, appropriate to the content and the learners?

- *Explaining*. When explaining principles and relating them to facts through examples, illustrations or analogies, does the teacher:

  - Define major concepts?
  - Give examples to illustrate these concepts?
  - Use examples that are accurate and concrete as well as abstract?

- *Presenting*. This refers to volume, pacing, articulation, and other speech mechanics. Does the teacher:

  - Articulate words clearly and project speech loudly enough?
  - Pace the sections of the presentation at rates conductive to understanding?
  - Support the verbal content with appropriate non-verbal communication and visual aids?

In summary, the whole class model of teaching includes the following five phases:

1 *Review*

- Review the concepts and skills from the previous lesson (and if appropriate the homework).

2 *Presenting information*

- Lecture or talk:

  - Pre-view the outline and scope of the lecture.
  - Introduce key terms or concepts.
  - Lecture proceeds in small steps, starting with what is familiar and using lively explanations and illustrations.

- Demonstration:

  - Preliminaries – a guide as to what to observe and expect.
  - Pre-view – purpose is outlined.
  - Rehearsal – teachers go through each step.
  - Reprise – procedures are repeated.

3 *Involving pupils in discussion*

- Focus on meaning and promoting student understanding through fast-paced discussion.
- Assess student comprehension through high-quality questioning.

4 *Engaging pupils in learning activities*

- Design activities to focus on content.
- Implementation of learning activities.

5 *Summary and review*

- Pupils ask follow-up questions, share findings and conclusions.
- Teacher reinforces key points, emphasizes central ideas and sums up achievements.

THE COOPERATIVE GROUP WORK TEACHING MODEL

As a model of teaching, cooperative group work has a powerful effect in raising pupil achievement because it harnesses the synergy of collective action. It combines the dynamics of democratic processes with the processes of academic enquiry. It encourages active participation in learning and collaborative behaviour by developing social as well as 'academic' skills. Thus the model requires pupils to practise and refine their negotiating, organizing and communication skills, define issues and problems, develop ways of solving them including collecting and interpreting evidence, hypothesizing, testing and re-evaluating.

The model is highly flexible and draws on a wide range of methods – individual research, collaborative enquiry and plenary activities – and allows the integration of them all into a powerful teaching tool. The teacher is able to conduct a more subtle and complex learning strategy that achieves a number of learning goals simultaneously. Thus, styles can vary from didactic to 'light touch' teaching where teacher is more an adviser and guide than a director. Two popular approaches to cooperative group learning are 'numbered heads' and the 'jigsaw'. Here are two examples of these approaches:

- *Numbered Heads* – In an English lesson the teacher is focusing on the punctuation of direct and indirect speech. First, the class is divided into named groups of four and each pupil is allocated a number. From a displayed passage of unpunctuated dialogue and description each group is asked to identify the direct speech. Everyone knows that after two minutes of discussion there will be silence signalled by a bell ringing and that one of them will have their number called and will have to respond. This motivates groups to share information and make sure everyone knows the answer. It gives every pupil a chance to shine and, because they have the group behind them, no one is made anxious about answering. Successful responses bolster both individual and collective confidence, which can be boosted further by some form of team award system.
- *Jigsaw* – In Food Technology a teacher sets up a question or problem for enquiry and divides pupils into equal-sized groups called Home Groups. Typical topics might include food hygiene in the home, safe practice in the kitchen, processed versus organic foodstuffs, dangerous additives and so on. Each group is given an identical task and suggested list of roles/jobs. For five minutes groups discuss the 'problem' and allocate roles/jobs. The Home groups then divide and those with identical jobs form new Expert groups whose function is to collect relevant information. After a period of research the original Home groups are reformed and expert knowledge pooled to solve the problem or map the issue.

There are many other examples of cooperative learning strategies (Hopkins and Harris 2000):

Twos to fours or snowballing – Children work together in pairs, perhaps upon a mathematical problem or science experiment. They then join with another pair to explain what they have achieved, and to compare this with the work of the other pair. This provides a valuable opportunity to express understanding, and to respond to the views of others in a supportive context.

Rainbow groups – A way of ensuring that children experience working alongside a range of others is to give each child in a group a number, or a colour.

When the group has worked together, all the children of the same number or colour form new groups to compare what they have done.

Envoys – Often, in group work, the teacher is concerned that she will be under pressure from many different directions. Envoying helps children to find help and support without necessarily having recourse to the teacher. If a group needs to check something, or to obtain information, one of the group can be sent as an 'envoy' to the library, or book corner, or another group, and then will report back. Another use is to ask groups to send an envoy to a different group to explain what they have done, obtain responses and suggestions, and bring them back to the group.

Listening triads – This strategy encourages children, in groups of three, to take on the roles of talker, questioner or recorder. The talker explains or comments on an issue or activity. The questioner prompts and seeks clarification. The recorder makes notes, and at the end of the (brief) time, gives a report of the conversation. Next time the roles are changed.

Critical friends – A group member is responsible for observing the ways in which the group works together. Using a simple guide list (which children can devise), the observer watches and listens as the children work. The group then discusses this information. This helps children to develop their own evaluative strategies.

Effective group work involves an agreed set of ground rules that are based on self-respect for individuals and directed at creating efficient working patterns. These ground rules are negotiated as part of an introductory all-class session and refined by each group afterwards to suit their particular concerted needs. Framed as negatives or positives these 'commandments' should establish norms of civilized and democratic behaviour and if developed collaboratively will be accepted and followed more readily. The rules should be simple, reasonable and just. They include, for example:

- No one should interrupt another.
- No one should abuse another.
- No one should ignore another.
- Criticism must be justified and evidenced.
- Different opinions should be respected.
- Praise should be given.
- All members should offer help and share knowledge.

For cooperative methods of learning to be effective, they have to be planned, implemented and monitored very carefully. An ideological commitment to the idea is not enough and, indeed, can result in poorly conceived group activities that may quickly become a shambles. Whilst cooperative methods have an enormous potential for encouraging success in the classroom, this is unlikely to be the outcome unless they are introduced in a systematic and coordinated way. Facilitating effective small group learning means helping group members perceive the importance of working together and interacting in helpful ways.

In summary, there are a wide range of strategies that comprise the cooperative group work teaching model. They are all however underpinned by the following principles (Johnson and Johnson 1993).

- *Positive interdependence* – When all members of a group feel connected to each other in the accomplishment of a common goal. All individuals must succeed for the group to succeed.
- *Individual accountability* – Holding every member of the group responsible to demonstrate the accomplishment of the learning.
- *Face-to-face interaction* – When group members are close in proximity to each other and enter into a dialogue with each other in ways that promote continued progress.
- *Social skills* – Human interaction skills that enable groups to function effectively (e.g. taking turns, encouraging, listening, giving help, clarifying, checking, understanding, probing). Such skills enhance communication, trust, leadership, decision making, and conflict management.
- *Processing* – When group members assess their collaborative efforts and target improvements.

THE INDUCTIVE TEACHING MODEL

Inductive teaching is a teaching model from the information processing family. Its main purpose is to encourage pupils to build, test and to use categories to organize their thinking about a particular topic or subject area.

> A year 10 class is being introduced to different styles of portrait painting as part of their GCSE course. Initially the teacher gives each individual an A4 handout containing numbered photographs of different kinds of portraits. The portraits represent a range of styles and are from different centuries. For five minutes, the teacher gets the class to look at the photographs individually. The class is then divided into pairs and the teacher instructs each pair to categorize the portraits by grouping certain photographs together using the numbers to group the categories. The pairs set about this task placing the portraits into groups and giving each category a name. The teacher makes it clear that some portraits could be placed in

several categories. She also reassures the pupils by telling them that any categories that can be named and justified are acceptable.

After 15 minutes or so, the teacher pauses this activity and asks several of the pairs to share their classification with the whole class and their reasons for classifying the portraits in this way. The pairs offer a series of numbers that are written up by the teacher for the whole class to view. While this is happening, other pupils look at their own classifications to ascertain whether they have reached similar conclusions or not. Having provided a set of numbers the other pupils are then asked by the teacher to guess the rationale behind the classification. One pair offers 'seventeenth century' as one category while another offers 'cubism' as a category. Eventually the initiators of the classification are asked to tell the class why they grouped the data together and the teacher helps the whole class look for links between the data chosen.

After several pairs have provided their categories and the class has worked out their reasons for grouping the data together, the teacher then hands each pair some additional photographs of portraits. The pairs are then asked to reconsider their categories with respect to the new data. The pupils are given time to allocate the new data within existing categories, or to re-categorize the whole data set. Once they have done this task the teacher once again asks selected pairs to share their classification and the labels they have given each category.

The teacher lists the different categories and asks the pupils to add any categories not represented by the list. The teacher then asks the pupils to choose one category and to paint a portrait in this style.

The inductive teaching model is a powerful way of helping pupils to learn how to construct knowledge. The model focuses directly on intellectual capability and is intended to assist pupils in the process of mastering large amounts of information. Within teaching there are numerous occasions when pupils are required to sort and classify data. However, in many cases the sorting process is viewed as an end in itself. Pupils are usually required to understand the 'one correct way of classifying'. Teachers know that there are usually many ways of classifying but they choose one for simplicity. The inductive method allows pupils to understand a variety of classifications in a structured way that includes a variety of teaching techniques within one method. Without opportunity for re-classification or hypothesizing, learning potential is limited and the development of high-order thinking is restricted.

The inductive model of teaching consists of a number of discrete phases that cannot be rushed or omitted. Inductive inquiries are rarely brief because the very nature of the inquiry requires pupils to think deeply.

The key activity in the inductive model is the collecting and sifting of information in order to construct categories or labels. This process requires pupils to engage with the data and seek to produce categories in which to allocate the data. It requires them to generate hypotheses based upon this allocation and to test out these hypotheses by using them to guide subsequent work.

The flow of the inductive model involves:

- Identifying the information relevant to a topic or a problem.
- Grouping individual items into categories that have common attributes.
- Classifying the information and developing labels for the categories. This also involves identifying and exploring critical relationships and making inferences.
- Creating hypotheses and predicting consequences.

The inductive teaching model follows a sequence of different phases. In the first phase pupils are presented with information or data sets and are required to sort the data into categories. The data sets are derived from a subject area and are intended to facilitate learning about a particular topic or theme. The data sets can be assembled by the teacher in advance of the lesson or collected by the pupils with guidance from the teacher. If assembled by the teacher, the data sets will be prepared with certain concepts in mind. To engage pupils in this model, teachers need to begin by presenting data sets to them and in subsequent lessons encouraging pupils to create and generate their own data sets. It is important that pupils have experience of the inductive model in all its phases and have success in learning with this model before embarking upon more sophisticated and complicated data sets.

To be really effective, data classification needs to occur several times. The initial phase of the classification is particularly important because this is where concepts are generated and applied. Following this initial phase, additional data or new information may be added that requires some reclassification or refinement of the categories. Adding new data means that concepts are challenged requiring pupils to think again about their initial classification. Through this iterative process pupils obtain control over the data and can understand related concepts more readily.

Inductive teaching increases pupils' ability to form concepts and to create linkages between different concepts. It also enables pupils to have a wider perspective on the topic in question and to think more broadly about the subject matter. Another, important aspect of the inductive model is the collective nature of the enquiry and the group responsibility to contribute to the compilation of categories. By allowing individuals to share their ideas with the whole class, different perspectives on the same data and challenges to thinking are inevitable.

There are many other advantages to the use of the model:

- It engages pupils in higher-order thinking;
- It involves variety in that the stages are taught in different ways so it supports a variety of learning styles;
- Once the data has been prepared, it can be easily kept from one year to another and its tangibility means that it is likely to get incorporated into schemes of work;
- Once the data has been prepared, it is easy to share amongst members of staff and across different schools;
- Providing teachers keep to the stages of the model, it provides a varied and stimulating way to learn.

In summary, the inductive model of teaching involves the following six phases (Joyce and Calhoun 1998):

- *Phase One: Identify the domain*
  - Establish the focus and boundaries of the initial inquiry.
  - Clarify the long-term objectives.

- *Phase Two: Collect, present, and enumerate data*
  - Assemble and present the initial data set.
  - Enumerate and label the items of data.

- *Phase Three: Examine data*
  - Thoroughly study the items in the data set and identify their attributes.

- *Phase Four: Form concepts by classifying*
  - Classify the items in the data set and share the results
  - Add data to the set.
  - Reclassification occurs, possibly many times.

- *Phase Five: Generate and test hypotheses*
  - Examine the implications of differences between categories.
  - Classify categories, as appropriate.
  - Reclassify in two-way matrices, as well as by correlations, as appropriate.

- *Phase Six: Consolidate and transfer*
  - Search for additional items of data in resource material.
  - Synthesize by writing about the domain, using the categories.
  - Convert categories into skills.
  - Test and consolidate skills through practice and application.

A BRIEF NOTE ON THE NATURE OF TEACHING STYLE

The concept of 'teaching style' has been well documented in the literature (see for example the series of studies by Bennett 1976, 1988, and Galton and his colleagues 1980, 1999). Instead of focusing on discrete teacher behaviour, as does the 'process – product' research associated with specific teacher effects, this research explores the relative effectiveness of different teaching styles or collections of teacher behaviours. An attempt has been made in the analysis of teaching given in this chapter to reflect the contribution of both schools of research to an understanding of effective teaching and learning.

The perspectives on high-quality teaching described in this chapter are not discrete; it is the practice of fine teachers to combine these elements through a process of reflection to create an individual style. Consequently, it may be that critical systematic reflection is a necessary condition for quality teaching. This is not reflection for reflection's sake, but in order to continue to develop a mastery of one's chosen craft.

Ultimately, however, effective teaching and learning has to be seen within a holistic framework. The comparative study of policies aimed at improving teacher quality we conducted for the OECD identified six characteristics of high-quality teachers (Hopkins and Stern 1996: 10):

- commitment,
- love of children,
- mastery of subject didactics,
- a repertoire of multiple models of teaching,
- the ability to collaborate with other teachers,
- a capacity for reflection.

Although it is convenient to group teachers' desired capacities and behaviours into categories, these attributes all interact in practice. For example, one French teacher elegantly defined teacher quality as 'savoirs, savoir-faire, et savoir-être', this is translatable perhaps as 'knowledge, knowing how to do, and knowing how to be' (Hopkins and Stern 1996: 503).

Finally, a comment on the debate around whether 'whole class' or 'group activity' should dominate, or what should be the balance between whole class, small group, and individual activities. Settling that question leads to the broader question of what will work best for children, because it is the models of learning and teaching that are chosen, rather than the grouping arrangements adopted, that will directly affect student achievement. In these classes, students are taught directly models for learning that they use when working as members of the class community, when working in small collaborative groups, and when working as individuals. The more efficient models of teaching assume that the whole class will be organized to pursue common learning objectives within which individual differences in achievement are comfortably accommodated. Thus, their creators have a vision of the whole class and a vision of small group work and individual work as part of the overall educational scheme (Joyce *et al.* 1997: 16).

Thus, as Bruce Joyce elegantly phrased it, the operational repertoire of the teacher is the critical element in the calculus of effects. One can teach whole classes well or badly, organize collaborative groups well or badly, and provide direct individual instruction well or badly, yet powerful teaching and learning occurs in powerful schools. As Lawrence Downey (1967) once put it: 'A school teaches in three ways, by what it teaches, by how it teaches and by the kind of place it is.' It is a consideration of the context and conditions that support effective teaching and learning that provide the focus for the following chapter.

FURTHER READING

Much of this chapter has been based on our previous writing on teaching and learning. The key text here is *Models of Teaching* (Joyce and Weil 1996). In *Models of Learning – Tools for Teaching* (Joyce *et al.* 2002), we adapted the original manuscript for a trans-American audience, and *Creating the Conditions for Teaching and Learning* (Hopkins and Harris 2000) reports on the use of these materials in IQEA schools. In terms of the different models of teaching described in this chapter, further information on whole class teaching can be found in Good and Brophy (1997) and Creemers (1994); on cooperative group work Sharan and Shachar (1988) and Johnson and Johnson (1993) are the most accessible sources; and on inductive teaching Joyce and Calhoun's (1997) *Learning to Teach Inductively* is mandatory. The literature on how children learn (Wood 1998), the different types or 'multiple intelligences' (Gardner 1991, 1993) and the descriptions of a range of learning styles (Kolb 1984) is helpful in designing increasingly effective learning experiences within authentic school improvement contexts. Useful sources for the research on teaching also includes Kyriacou (1997, 1998) and Miujs and Reynolds (2001), together with the other studies reported earlier in this chapter.

CHAPTER 11

Development planning, classroom research and school improvement

Since the end of the 1980s, the amount of change expected of teachers and schools has increased enormously. As well as the curriculum and organizational changes with which we are all too familiar, there are also a number of central policy initiatives in England and Wales that are potentially supportive of teacher and school development. Whether by accident or design, changes in the funding and delivery of staff development, schemes for school self-evaluation, appraisal and performance management, and school development planning are all supportive of what David Hargreaves (1994) called the 'new professionalism'. With a little imagination, all of these activities can combine or 'braid' together to form an 'infrastructure' at the school level to support the management of change and the professional development of teachers.

The days when schools had to contend with single innovations are long gone. These are times of innovation overload, when multiple changes have to be managed simultaneously, and we have to learn new strategies to cope with constant and complex change. In our experience, the essential strategy consists in selecting areas for action, in finding connections between these areas, and in ensuring that there is an adequate infrastructure to support the strategy. This infrastructure is composed of the links between strategies such as staff development and planning on the one hand, and the classroom research and teaching skills of staff on the other. Our more successful schools exploit innovation, they take the opportunity of the recent changes and use them to support developments already underway or planned for in the school. In short, they adapt external change for internal purpose.

Looking across all of these 'developmental changes', a major common denominator is classroom research. Classroom observation in particular is a fundamental strategy for school self-evaluation, performance management, development planning, as well as curriculum development and the acquisition of new teaching strategies. Our school improvement experience convinces me of the crucial role classroom observation and research can play in supporting the professional growth of teachers and the process of school development.

In this chapter, I discuss ways in which classroom observation and research can support teacher development and school improvement, with particular reference to school development planning. After a brief discussion of school self-evaluation, I concentrate on an approach to development planning that emphasizes the achievement of pupils and the role of the teacher's professional judgement in that process. I conclude the chapter by discussing how these various activities can combine to create a school-based approach to educational change that supports the achievement of students and the work of teachers.

SCHOOL SELF-EVALUATION

Perhaps the most obvious and longstanding link with classroom research has been the relationship with school self-evaluation. In the 1980s, teacher research and school self-evaluation were regarded as the two sides of the same coin. They both provide the opportunity whereby teachers and schools can obtain a degree of autonomy within the educational system. Classroom research emancipates (to use Stenhouse's word) teachers from authoritative forms of knowledge, theory and policy; and school self-evaluation – and more recently school development planning – enable a school to take more control of its curriculum and organization and plan its future more effectively and independently. Both activities also share a common set of procedures, which relate to a self-conscious and systematic attempt to review what they (both as individuals and as organizations) are doing and to proceed to action based on that analysis.

Local education authority (LEA) schemes for school self-evaluation or school-based review became very popular in the early to mid-1980s. By the middle of 1982, for example, four-fifths of the LEAs in England and Wales had devised schemes for systematic school-based review. These schemes had one major feature in common: virtually all included a booklet of classified questions or statements about schools and schooling. For reasons that I describe briefly below, school self-evaluation lost popularity during the late 1980s and early 1990s, but is now enjoying a renaissance due to its links with new forms of inspection and John Macbeath's work on self-evaluation and school ethos (Macbeath 1999).

Perhaps the best known of the schemes for school self-evaluation was 'GRIDS', which began as a Schools Council project based at the University of Bristol. The focus of GRIDS is the internal development of schools.

GRIDS was designed to help teachers to review and develop the curriculum and organization of their school, and two practical handbooks – one primary, one secondary – were produced for the purpose (McMahon *et al.* 1984). In its second stage, GRIDS was modified in order to recognize the need to be externally accountable, widen the roles of those who contribute to a review, assist with the identification of in-service needs and the management of change. New materials were also developed to assist teachers in establishing criteria for effectiveness and in using GRIDS in secondary schools at the department level (Abbott *et al.* 1988).

The central practical recommendation in the GRIDS method was that the staff should not attempt to make a detailed review of all aspects of the school at once. Instead, they should take a broad look at what is happening in the school, on the basis of this identify one or two areas that they consider to be priorities for specific review and development, tackle these first, evaluate what they have achieved, and then select another priority. The process was broken down into a series of key steps and tasks that have a logical structure, and a systematic step-by-step approach was recommended throughout. The five stages in this cyclical problem-solving process are outlined in Figure 11.1. It is described here because it still represents an excellent example of a generic problem-solving cycle.

Stage 1, getting started, is where preliminary decisions have to be made about whether or not the GRIDS method would be appropriate for the school and, if so, how it should be managed. The purpose of stage 2, the initial review, is to identify the topics that the staff consider to be priorities for specific review and development. Stage 3 is a specific review of the topics that have been identified as priorities; it entails a careful examination of current practice and an assessment of its effectiveness before making recommendations about development. Stage 4 is the action stage, when the recommendations are put into practice. Stage 5, overview and restart, is where evaluation of the development work and of the whole process takes place, and a new cycle of review and development begins.

Our own assessment of self-evaluation work suggested that schools find carrying out a full review of all provision and practice very time consuming (Hopkins 1987). In the past, schemes of school-based review demanded a thorough examination of the life and work of the school and two or three terms were often set aside for this. Today, the pressure for change makes this approach less appropriate. We proposed that this energy is now best used in carrying out a series of small-scale focused or specific 'audits' in key areas and in implementing the action plans that may result from these enquiries. A planned series of specific audits creates a rolling programme that provides a picture of the school built up over successive years (Hargreaves and Hopkins 1991).

We also found that there was an apparent lack of rigour and objectivity in many review and development procedures, and perhaps more

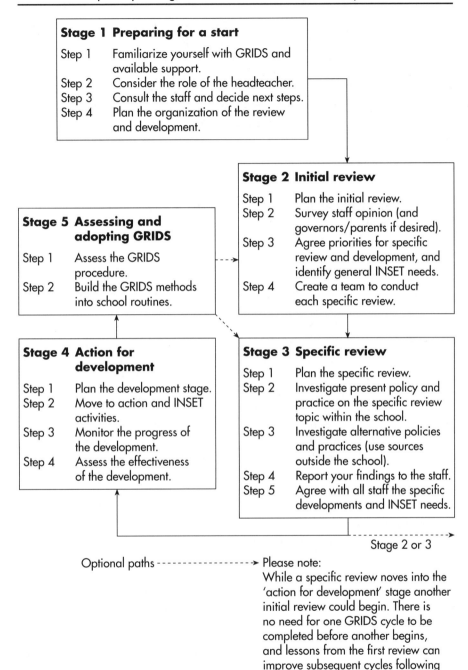

Stage 1 Preparing for a start

Step 1   Familiarize yourself with GRIDS and available support.
Step 2   Consider the role of the headteacher.
Step 3   Consult the staff and decide next steps.
Step 4   Plan the organization of the review and development.

Stage 2 Initial review

Step 1   Plan the initial review.
Step 2   Survey staff opinion (and governors/parents if desired).
Step 3   Agree priorities for specific review and development, and identify general INSET needs.
Step 4   Create a team to conduct each specific review.

Stage 5 Assessing and adopting GRIDS

Step 1   Assess the GRIDS procedure.
Step 2   Build the GRIDS methods into school routines.

Stage 4 Action for development

Step 1   Plan the development stage.
Step 2   Move to action and INSET activities.
Step 3   Monitor the progress of the development.
Step 4   Assess the effectiveness of the development.

Stage 3 Specific review

Step 1   Plan the specific review.
Step 2   Investigate present policy and practice on the specific review topic within the school.
Step 3   Investigate alternative policies and practices (use sources outside the school).
Step 4   Report your findings to the staff.
Step 5   Agree with all staff the specific developments and INSET needs.

Stage 2 or 3

Optional paths - - - - - - - - - - - - - - - - →   Please note:
While a specific review noves into the 'action for development' stage another initial review could begin. There is no need for one GRIDS cycle to be completed before another begins, and lessons from the first review can improve subsequent cycles following closely behind.

Figure 11.1   The GRIDS cycle. Reproduced with the permission of SCDC Publications.

importantly school self-evaluation had difficulty in impacting directly on classroom practice. If the staff involved in GRIDS and similar evaluations had been experienced in classroom research, not only would the reviews have been more 'reliable', but closer links would have been established between the whole school evaluation and classroom practice. It was for these reasons that we began to advocate more comprehensive strategies for school improvement such as development planning, and as seen in the following sections designed these strategies around a focus that embraced both classroom practice and teacher development.

DEVELOPMENT PLANNING FOR PUPIL PROGRESS AND ACHIEVEMENT

Development planning has firmly established itself as a key strategy for school improvement since the 1990s. In England in 1989 when the then DES issued its first advice, development planning was regarded as a means of helping schools manage the extensive national and centrally driven change agenda, and to enable the school 'to organise what it is already doing and what it needs to do in a more purposeful and coherent way' (DES 1989: 4). Given the amount of change schools and teachers were expected to cope with in the late 1980s and early 1990s, such a strategy was welcomed by many (Hargreaves and Hopkins 1991).

The DES project on school development plans (SDP) began at a time (1989) when schools had to adjust to an increasingly centralized reform agenda. It was an attempt to develop a strategy that would, among other things, help schools manage the conflicting demands being placed on them. In its simplest form an SDP brings together, in an overall plan, national and LEA policies and initiatives, the school's aims and values, its existing achievements and needs for development, and enables it to organize what it is already doing and what it needs to do in a more purposeful and coherent way. By coordinating aspects that are otherwise separate, the school acquires a shared sense of direction and is able to control and manage the tasks of development and change. Priorities for development are planned in detail for one year and are supported by action plans that are the working documents for teachers. The priorities for subsequent years are sketched in outline to provide the longer term programme (Hargreaves *et al.* 1989: 4). An overview of the planning process is seen in Figure 11.2.

Research into school improvement during the 1990s indicated that during this decade the use of development planning itself changed in many schools (Hopkins *et al.* 1996; MacGilchrist *et al.* 1997). One research study in particular (MacGilchrist *et al.* 1995), showed that schools that exhibited best practice in development planning used it as a strategy to enhance directly the progress and achievement of students. The crucial difference

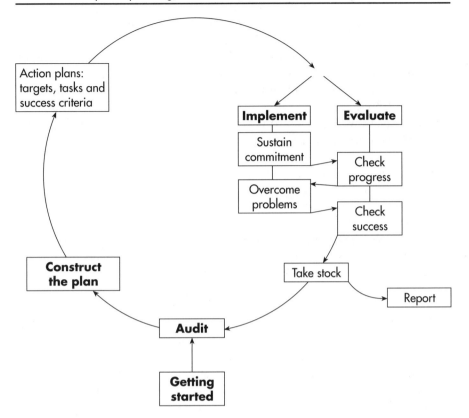

Figure 11.2 The planning process.

between this and previous approaches to development planning was that it was rooted in classrooms. The focus was on students' learning, their progress and achievement; what was needed to improve it and how this was best supported.

The plan begins with learning goals for students. A teaching strategy for achieving them is then produced. This strategy is supported by any necessary adjustments to the school's management arrangements: for example, modifications to curriculum policies and schemes of work, changes to the staff development programme and the timetable and any re-allocation of budgets, roles and responsibilities needed to achieve the goals set. This is radically different from the type of plan that simply focuses on the implementation of external change, however important that is, or on the development of school-wide policies and practices, which in themselves may not have a direct impact on classroom practice.

Evidence of good practice and the lessons of research suggest that development planning needs to focus both on how to accelerate the progress and enhance the achievement of students *as well as* establishing effective management practices within the school. This approach to planning is neither top-down – focused in the main on management arrangements – nor bottom-up – committed to specific changes in individual classrooms – but a combination of the two. It is this that has led to a reconceptualization of how development planning can be used to enhance pupil progress and achievement.

This 'new' approach to development planning concerns the integration of three key foci (Hopkins and MacGilchrist 1998):

- Pupil progress and achievement;
- The quality of teaching and learning;
- Management arrangements to support the first two.

Those schools that have identified clear learning targets for pupils use development planning to achieve these by concentrating *simultaneously* on related improvements inside and outside the classroom (Hopkins 2000). In particular:

- *Teaching* – they place particular emphasis on the content of teachers' planning and on the type of teaching strategies that will enable the learning goals for students to be achieved.
- *Management arrangements* – they identify any modifications that are needed to the school's current arrangements, for example, the timetable, the budget, staffing and staff development. They plan for any changes that may be needed in the school's curriculum policies and schemes of work and assessment arrangements.

Research emphasizes the importance of planning for these two kinds of improvement, and experience suggests that the stronger the relationship between them the more successful the school is in raising standards (MacGilchrist *et al.* 1995). In the past, for very understandable reasons, plans have tended to concentrate on management arrangements with the result that, for many schools, the plan had little significant impact on pupils' learning. The planning focused on staff activities rather than student outcomes. The key lesson is that when schools plan for both of these aspects of development in a strategic way it does make a difference where it matters most, namely in the classroom for pupils.

Figure 11.3 illustrates the interface between whole school development and classroom practice and the integration of these three foci (Hopkins and MacGilchrist 1998). At the heart is the pupils' progress and achievement supported by the quality of teaching and learning in the classroom. This is the core business of schools. Outside the classroom are the key management arrangements and practices that support and provide the context for quality learning experiences in the classroom.

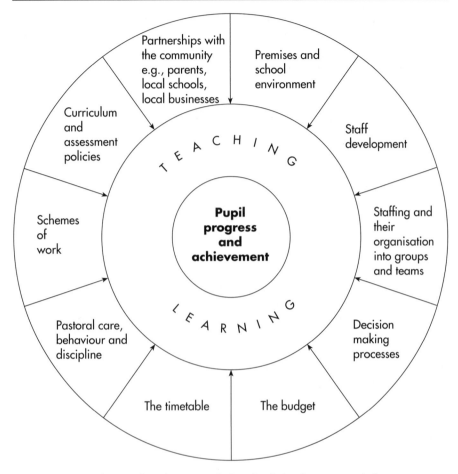

Figure 11.3 The interface between whole school development and classroom practice (from Hopkins and MacGilchrist 1998).

It is evident from OFSTED inspections and DfEE surveys of good practice that successful schools have established a rolling programme of policy review and revision spanning a number of years related to the particular priority for student learning and achievement being worked on at that point in time. This has given these schools the space to use the development plan to achieve an explicit classroom focus. They are able to choose priorities that:

- Focus on pupil progress and achievement;
- Are manageable and few in number;
- Relate to the school's vision;
- Are sequenced over time.

By using these and other similar criteria a school is able to establish a set of targets directly focused on pupils' learning and their achievement. It can then pay close attention to any improvements needed in the quality of teaching in the classroom and the implications of these for the management arrangements across the school as a whole. In this way the school's development plan has a central focus on specific aspects of teaching and learning and the conditions necessary to support these. This will inevitably have a 'knock on' effect for the timetable, the budget, staffing arrangements, INSET and possibly the premises. The schedules for these basic aspects of the work of the school will, therefore, need to take account of current and future priorities in the development plan.

In any action plan for student achievement the classroom should therefore be the main focus for improvement. The priorities for development must also be rooted in evidence about pupils' progress and achievement. Targeted action can then concern:

- Specific improvements in pupil outcomes;
- Changes in teaching practices;
- Any modifications needed to school-wide provision and management arrangements to support developments in the classroom.

An action plan for student achievement will therefore need to include the following (Hopkins and MacGilchrist 1998):

- *Specific* targets related to *pupils'* learning, progress and achievement that are clear and unambiguous;
- *Teaching and learning strategies* designed to meet the targets;
- *Evidence* to be gathered to judge the success in achieving the targets set;
- Modifications to *management arrangements* to enable targets to be met;
- *Tasks* to be done to achieve the targets set and who is responsible for doing them;
- *Time* it will take;
- How much it will *cost* in terms of the budget, staff time, staff development and other resources;
- *Responsibility* for *monitoring* the implementation of the plan;
- *Evaluating* its impact over time.

As distinct from previous approaches that focused on the management of external change and the implementation of school-wide policies, this approach to development planning begins with the learning needs of students and moves out from there. After setting targets for student learning, progress and achievement, the plan focuses on developing a strategy for enhancing teaching and creating powerful learning experiences; and then on the management arrangements required to support such changes in classroom practice.

In reality, both these aspects of the school's development plan coalesce in practice. They are also grounded in and supported by other forms of planning in the school.

ENHANCING THE PROFESSIONAL JUDGEMENT OF TEACHERS

We have previously (Ainscow *et al.* 2000: 11) set out the case for enquiry-driven improvement efforts:

> We have observed that those schools which recognise that enquiry and reflection are important processes in school improvement find it easier to sustain improvement effort around established priorities, and are better placed to monitor the extent to which policies actually deliver the intended outcomes for pupils. Central to the conditions, which promote the effective use of enquiry and reflection as developmental tools, are:
>
> - Systematic collection, interpretation and use of school-generated data in decision-making.
> - Effective strategies for reviewing the progress and impact of school policies and initiatives.
> - Widespread involvement of staff in the processes of data collection and analysis.
> - Clear ground rules for the collection, control and use of school-based data.

Unfortunately, in a large number of schools the range of data available is being underused. Of course, some schools are much better organized in this area, and have clear systems and procedures for collecting, analysing and interpreting information which is seen as relevant to particular aspects of the school or particular decisions. Even in these cases, however, a more general commitment to enquire into and reflect on the school's progress is rare – more often it is the issue that is identified then the information collected, rather than data being collected to help identify what the issue should be.

I would not want to suggest here that everything that takes place in a school can be noted, nor that all information has equal significance. But our work with schools that have adopted a sustained commitment to improvement initiatives has led us to identify the habits of enquiry and reflection as important forces for improvement. Schools that, for example, have experienced success at development planning have checked regularly on progress. By doing this staff ensure that the implementation of the action plan is kept on track, is of high quality, and that necessary adjustments are made as action proceeds.

As has already been noted, the key to the integration of implementation and evaluation of school improvement activities is the action plan used by groups of teachers. An action plan is a working document that describes and summarizes what needs to be done to implement and evaluate a priority. It serves as a guide to implementation and helps to monitor progress and success. There are three key elements to the enquiry aspect of the action plan:

1 the *success criteria* against which progress and success in reaching targets can be judged;
2 the allocation of responsibility to *assess progress*;
3 how *success* is subsequently judged.

Teachers often find defining the success criteria the most difficult part of the action plan. It is much easier to break down a priority into targets and tasks than it is to define success criteria. As we noted in *The Empowered School* (Hargreaves and Hopkins 1991: 50–51) targets must, however, specify the criteria by which success in reaching the target can be judged, both by team members and by others. These *success criteria* are a form of school-generated performance indicator, which:

• give *clarity* about the target: what exactly are you trying to achieve?;
• point to the *standard* expected by the team;
• provide advance warning of the *evidence* needed to judge successful implementation;
• give an indication of the *time-scale* involved.

The success criteria are a means for evaluating the outcomes of the plan, as well as providing benchmarks for development. It is important that they specify the minimal acceptable standard, though the team will usually have aspirations to a standard of outcome that is much higher than this.

At least once a term progress should be formally checked for each task against the success criteria associated with the target. We defined a *progress check* in *The Empowered School* (Hargreaves and Hopkins 1991: 67) as an act of evaluation *in the course of* implementation. It is a response to the question: how are we doing so far? Many progress checks are intuitive, a 'feel' for whether things are going well or badly. This is a natural part of monitoring one's activities: it becomes more systematic if these intuitive reactions are shared within the team, and evidence is produced to support them. Regular *progress checks* involve:

• giving somebody in the team responsibility for ensuring that the progress checks take place;

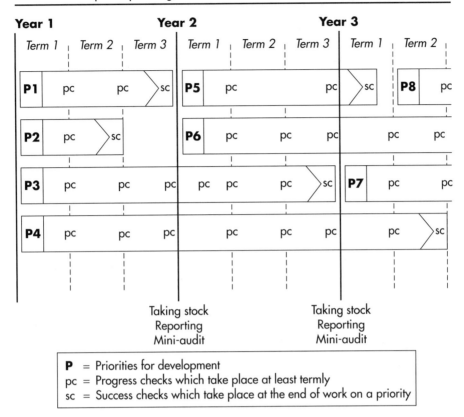

Figure 11.4 The relationship between progress and success checks in development planning (Hargreaves and Hopkins 1991: 68).

- reviewing progress at team meetings, especially when taking the next step forward or making decisions about future directions;
- deciding what will count as evidence of progress in relation to the success criteria;
- finding quick methods of collecting evidence from different sources;
- recording the evidence and conclusions for later use.

Success checks take place at the end of the developmental work on a target. The team now decides how successful the implementation of the target or priority as a whole has been. Checking success need not be complex or time-consuming. It will consist largely in collating, and then drawing a conclusion about, the earlier progress checks. The relationship between progress and success checks is represented diagrammatically in Figure 11.4.

In *The Empowered School* David Hargreaves and I argued that the process of checking on progress and success in development planning requires teachers to use their professional judgement in a systematic way (Hargreaves and Hopkins 1991: Ch 9). It is not the mechanistic completion of progress and success checks that is important, but rather it is the enhancing of the teachers' professional judgement that is the crucial aspect of embedding an ethos of enquiry and reflection within a school. This process provides the interface between development planning, classroom research and school improvement.

Teachers already, as part of their everyday activities, monitor and evaluate their own actions as well as the behaviour and work of pupils. If teachers did not rely on their *intuitive professional judgement,* they would not be able to cope with the complexities of their work. There are occasions, however, when it cannot be wholly relied on as a basis for making a decision. Such occasions are when teachers are not entirely confident about their intuitive judgement, or the issue is of considerable importance or significance. In these circumstances, teachers make a *considered professional judgement,* which requires some action to check the intuitive judgement. A considered professional judgement is reached through reflection and further investigation. Using *intuitive* and *considered* professional judgements is a routine part of being a teacher. Both are a natural and inherent part not only of assessing progress for evaluation but more generally as a key feature of the school improvement process.

Innovations often create new working circumstances with which the teacher is less familiar. Since teachers usually want the innovation to succeed, there may be a bias towards noticing the most favourable evidence. Professional judgement may therefore be less trustworthy than usual. In these cases a *refined professional judgement* is required. This is an opportunity for enhancing professional judgement, and is achieved:

- through discussion with colleagues about the extent of progress or success in school improvement work;
- by establishing agreement on standards used to make judgements;
- through mutual observation in the classroom;
- through the use of informed opinion.

When it is well structured, development work provides ample opportunities for teachers to talk with others, to seek agreement on standards, to observe one another and to read relevant documentation: all are means of refining the professional judgements which are so essential for evaluation and school improvement. It is here where the potential of evaluation as school improvement is realized. Extending teachers' professional judgements therefore links the professional development of the individual teacher to the development of the school as a whole as well as improving the quality of teaching and learning.

There are circumstances when teachers need to *complement* even a refined professional judgement with additional evidence. Such occasions are when others need to be persuaded of the validity of teachers' judgements, or when there are benefits to all if teachers' judgements are backed by independent evidence. Collecting complementary evidence is usually more time-consuming than making professional judgements, so careful thought needs to be given to questions such as: What kind of complementary evidence is appropriate to documenting success? How can it be collected as quickly and easily as possible without adding substantially to existing workloads? There are different types and sources of complementary evidence, and it is these that reflect what is often regarded as more formal approaches to evaluation:

- observations (e.g. mutual observation during teacher appraisal),
- views and opinions (e.g. short questionnaire to colleagues, students or parents),
- written materials (e.g. a 'book look' of students work),
- statistical information (e.g. trends in student attendance rates),
- more formal research (e.g. by a colleague on a 'masters' course).

To summarize, the formative evaluation of development planning is supported through the identification of success criteria and the use of regular progress and success checks. Although these frameworks are important in underpinning a process of evaluation process, it is the enhancing of the professional judgements of teachers that sustains and adds value to the process. As is seen in the following section it is the role of classroom research and the enquiry into teaching and learning that in the longer term positively affects the culture of the school.

LOCATING CLASSROOM RESEARCH WITHIN A MODEL OF SCHOOL IMPROVEMENT

Our 'Improving the Quality of Education For All' (IQEA) school improvement project, in common with a number of school improvement projects throughout the world, has sought to develop the capacity of schools to accommodate and use external change in order to maximize student outcomes. IQEA focuses on the teaching/learning process and the conditions that support it in the knowledge that, without an equal focus on the development capacity or internal conditions of the school, innovative classroom work will soon become marginalized. The IQEA project works from an assumption that schools are most likely to strengthen their ability to provide enhanced outcomes for all pupils when they adopt ways of working that are consistent with both their own and the current reform agenda. Indeed, the schools we are currently working with are using the external drive to improve teaching and learning as a basis for conducting their developmental work at the classroom level.

At the outset of IQEA we attempted to outline our own vision of school improvement by articulating a set of principles that provided us with a philosophical and practical starting point (Ainscow *et al.* 2000; Hopkins 2001a, 2002). These principles represent the expectations we have of the way project schools pursue school improvement. They serve as an *aide-mémoire* to the schools and to ourselves. We feel that the operation of these principles creates synergism – together they are greater than the sum of their parts.

- School improvement is a process that focuses on enhancing the *quality of students' learning*.
- The vision of the school should be one which embraces *all* members of the school community as both learners and contributors.
- The school will secure its *internal priorities* through adopting external pressures for change and in so doing enhance its capacity for managing change.
- the school will seek to use data, action research and *enquiry* to drive forward and inform with school improvement efforts.
- the school will seek to develop structures and create conditions that encourage collaboration and lead to the *empowerment* of students and teachers.

From the experience within the IQEA project we have identified a number of 'conditions' at school and classroom level that support and sustain school improvement (Ainscow *et al.* 2000; Hopkins 2002). At school level, these conditions provide a working definition of the *development capacity* of the school. They represent the key management arrangements and can be broadly stated as:

- a commitment to staff development,
- practical efforts to involve staff, students and the community in school policies and decisions,
- 'transformational' leadership approaches,
- effective coordination strategies,
- proper attention to the potential benefits of enquiry and reflection,
- a commitment to collaborative planning activity.

These conditions are the internal features of the school that enable the work to get done. At the classroom level also, a set of conditions exist that facilitate and sustain effective teaching and learning (Hopkins *et al.* 1998). Schools working within IQEA are encouraged to work on the school level and classroom level conditions simultaneously.

In our recent cohorts, schools within the project have sought to integrate work at both levels by focusing on different models of teaching in order to expand teacher's instructional repertoires. There is mounting evidence that the content of a lesson notwithstanding, the use of appropriate teaching strategies can significantly increase student achievement. A major goal for school improvement, therefore, is to help teachers become professionally flexible so that they can select, from a repertoire of possibilities, the teaching approach most suited to their particular content area, and the age, interests and aptitudes of their students. One of the characteristics of successful schools is that teacher's talk about teaching. In IQEA schools this involves:

- teachers discussing with each other the nature of teaching strategies;
- establishing specifications or guidelines for the chosen teaching strategies;
- agreeing on standards used to assess student progress as a result;
- mutual observation and partnership teaching in the classroom.

This focus has provided a basis for staff development and planning at the school level, as well as peer observation and innovation in the classroom. Having selected a particular model of teaching, each school places priority on embedding the model into the teachers' classroom practice. When this has been achieved, other models are subsequently added to further enhance the quality of teaching and learning within the school. This experience suggests that focusing on models of teaching has enabled IQEA schools to build the capacity for change at both the school and classroom levels. It has also created a coherent programme of staff development within IQEA schools that impacts directly and positively on student achievement and learning. It is the recent focus on models of teaching in IQEA schools that provides the focus of the following example.

Swanwick Hall School is an 11–18 comprehensive school in eastern Derbyshire with a fully comprehensive intake but a skew to the less able. The school joined the East Midlands IQEA partnership in 1997 because many of the 'school improvement measures' used in school prior to that time were not classroom based. Ruth Watts, the deputy head, describes what this emphasis on teaching and learning has meant:

- A better deal for pupils in terms of interest and variety, which caters for a greater range of learning styles.
- Most staff development time has been concentrated on teaching and learning which pleased virtually all staff.
- The impetus for change belongs to a volunteer group of staff ranging across departments and experience (it includes the head teacher and several NQTs) working collaboratively with the heads of faculty group. This means that the staff does not feel driven by

senior management or external pressures as much as they did previously.

After extensive discussion, the IQEA group decided that all staff should concentrate on the model of inductive teaching for the first year of development. The main reasons for this decision were:

- The model is applicable to all departments.
- No one understood it previously so all staff were learning together and sharing ideas across departments.
- The different phases cater for different styles of teaching, including individual and group work, so there is variety in the lessons.
- The six phases make it quite a complex model, which requires understanding, so the staff had something to talk about. Comments were heard like 'Phases 1–4 are fine but then I struggle with phases 5 and 6. Any ideas?'
- The latter phases involve higher order thinking skills, which were underdeveloped in school at the time.
- Though the data for inductive teaching often requires considerable time in planning, it can be used from year to year, once it exists. This has meant that building the teaching model into schemes of work has not been too difficult.

Once the volunteer group had practised the model and videoed themselves, they were ready to organize a whole school inservice day with time to learn about the model and then prepare work for inductive teaching in departments. Volunteer staff, who had never done any Inset work before, talked to the rest of the staff at the following training day. This produced a much more powerful message than an expert from outside school.

Over the next 12 months a variety of ways were found to share ideas on inductive teaching:

- More half inset days to report back on progress and develop more data sets for new lessons.
- There was co-planning and co-teaching while the volunteer IQEA group covered colleagues' lessons.
- Ideas and strategies were shared via videos.
- After every staff development session, each department completed a questionnaire for the IQEA group who published a 'State of Inductive teaching' report for staff.
- Lists were produced of topics taught inductively, with lists of the year groups involved. These ranged from Year 7 to Year 13 with no obvious bias to any particular key stage.

- Heads of faculty meetings were used as ways of sharing ideas and problems, e.g. how to include reluctant staff, building the model into schemes of work.
- Students were questioned about their perceptions of teaching and learning and the results were published.
- A year later the inservice day was started with a 'curriculum tour', that is all departments put on a 20-minute workshop on topics they had taught inductively. This again proved to be a highly successful staff development session.

The IQEA group accepted some flexibility during the year. The languages department, for example, decided that many Key Stage 3 pupils needed more vocabulary in order for inductive teaching to work. So they made a decision to start with mnemonics, prior to moving into inductive teaching. This worked very well for them. One or two departments were slower to start than others for internal reasons but, on the whole, staff felt that inductive teaching was an ideal way for Swanwick Hall to start the IQEA journey.

The pattern for the second year of IQEA was very similar to the first. The focus for Year 2 was cooperative group work and mnemonics, while remembering that it was still important to check that inductive teaching was well embedded into schemes of work. Virtually all departments engaged in cooperative group work, especially pairs/fours, jigsaw techniques and numbered heads. As part of the process staff uniformly decided where students were to sit, so that it was far easier to organize group work than previously. Some very committed staff moved students around so often that they now ask, 'Where do you want us to sit today?' as they enter the room. Staff worked hard to establish cooperative learning standards, with an ethos of acceptance of all contributions.

Mnemonics was the other new work for Year 2. As a model it is much quicker to learn than inductive teaching and cooperative group work but it suits staff with creative minds more than those who struggle to devise interesting mnemonics. It has been used extensively in languages and science with several other departments trying it. Sometimes the pupils are much better than the staff and produce excellent mnemonics.

The third year of IQEA was more open-ended. Departments felt increasingly self-confident in developing their own variety in teaching and learning. Several departments are using synectics, and concept attainment has worked well in 'content heavy' courses. The maths department has improved its approach to investigations in maths. The languages department is heavily involved in preferred learning styles with techniques for ensuring there is more kinaesthetic learning, as well as the use of audio and visual aids. Some of the scientists are using accelerated learning techniques. Monitoring progress and sharing ideas has been harder but only because the impetus for development comes from departments and individual teachers rather than being centrally controlled.

Future plans for school improvement at Swanwick include:

- To develop the use of some of the newer models across more staff.
- Linking work on behaviour for learning more specifically to the IQEA initiative.
- Using the 'cooperative learning standards' more widely together with some of the ideas from accelerated learning.
- Collecting more data from staff and pupils about progress and perceptions.
- Increasing the number of staff able to give workshops on teaching and learning to other schools in the networks. (During the academic year 2000–01 over 20 staff have been involved in delivering school improvement workshops around England and Wales, and even as far away as Hong Kong!)

It is in these ways that successful schools such as Swanwick Hall are pursuing their improvement efforts. These schools are now using their development plans to improve pupil achievement and progress in a much more explicit way. Their school improvement is about raising student achievement through focusing on the quality of teaching and learning in classrooms, and the management arrangements that support it. There are three key messages from this example and the evidence of research and practice that provide insights into how to do this.

1 *Keep the focus on student learning* The increasing national emphasis on student academic outcomes is very welcome. There is a danger however that the focus on SAT scores, and GCSE and A level results will concentrate attention on attainment at the expense of the quality of pupils' learning. Achievement at whatever level is based on pupils' ability to respond effectively to the tasks they are set, and this depends on how well they can take control over their own learning (Mortimore 1993). It is these skills and strategies as well as the focus on academic outcomes that need to become integrated into the targets a school sets itself for pupil progress and achievement.

2 *Maintain consistency across the school* Schools that add value to the learning, progress and attainment of their pupils are consistent in their teaching practices, the educational values that they hold, the high levels of expectation that they have and their low tolerance of failure. Pupils in highly effective schools are clear about what is required from them, feel secure

in their learning and school environment, and respond positively to the academic and social demands placed upon them.

3 *Clarify the link between effective teaching and student learning outcomes* Effective teachers and effective schools take seriously the link between classroom practice and student learning outcomes; particularly in terms of what the students learn, how the students learn, the pace of learning and the high expectations existing in the classroom. Teaching strategies reflect not just the teacher's classroom management skills, but also the ability of the teacher to help students to acquire new knowledge through, for example, learning how to extract information from presentations, to memorize information, to build hypotheses and concepts, to use metaphors to think creatively, and to work effectively with others to initiate and carry out cooperative tasks (Joyce *et al.* 1997).

In conclusion, school improvement as an approach to educational change is concerned with school process as well as student outcomes; it is about enhancing teaching and learning as well as the conditions that support it. So those who work in the field of school improvement actively seek to enhance student outcomes through specific changes in teaching approaches, and through strengthening the school's culture and its organizational ability to support the work of teachers. As I hope has become apparent in the last two chapters, teacher-researchers have a key role to play in these developments.

FURTHER READING

This chapter has touched on a broad range of issues that has a vast supporting literature. As regards school self-evaluation, the GRIDS handbooks (Abbott *et al.* 1988; McMahon *et al.* 1984) and Macbeath's (1999) work are essential reading. Of interest also are Phil Clift and colleagues' (1987) *Studies in School Self Evaluation*, as well as our own work on school-based review (Bollen and Hopkins 1987; Hopkins 1987, 1988). The link between school self-evaluation and inspection is described in an OFSTED booklet (OFSTED 1998). Our research on development planning resulted in the DES booklet *Planning for School Development* (Hargreaves *et al.* 1989), *The Empowered School* (Hargreaves and Hopkins 1991) and the more recent reconceptualization of development planning around a central focus on teaching and learning and student achievement (Hargreaves and Hopkins 1994; Hopkins and MacGilchrist 1998). The work of Barbara MacGilchrist and her colleagues at the institute of Education, London has been both helpful and insightful, in particular *Planning Matters* (1995) and *The Intelligent School* (1997). Our own work on school improvement, on which much of this chapter has been based, provides research accounts and tools, handbooks and training materials, as well as more academic reviews (Ainscow *et al.* 2000; Beresford 1998; Hopkins 2001, 2002; Hopkins *et al.* 1994, 1996, 1997, 1998). Finally, the literature on school improvement in general is also growing. Comprehensive treatments are found in *The New Structure of School Improvement* (Joyce *et al.* 1999), *Innovation and Change* (Rudduck 1991), *What's Worth Fighting For?* series (Fullan and Hargreaves 1992; Hargreaves and Fullan 1998), *Changing our Schools* (Stoll and Fink 1996) and *Change Forces* (Fullan 1993). Last but by no means least, the standard texts on educational change are Michael Fullan's (2001) *The New Meaning of Educational Change* (third edition), and *The International Encyclopaedia of Educational Change* in four volumes (Hargreaves *et al.* 1998).

CHAPTER 12

Teacher research and the creation of professional learning communities

In his evocative essay, *The Tree*, John Fowles (1979) talks of the importance of 'seeing nature whole'. He argues against the contemporary reductionist and utilitarian view of the environment that alienates us from the source of nature itself. By fragmenting nature, by categorizing it, by breaking it up into little pieces so that we can 'understand it', we lose its essence. The more we try to control nature in this way, the more we move away from and fail to grasp its vital spirit. So it is with teacher development. The more we regard teachers as functionaries, the more we move towards reductionist notions of 'competency' and dull the spark of creative artistry, the more we impoverish the teaching and learning in our schools.

Much has changed in education since the first edition of this book was published. Although many of the changes are to be welcomed, not all of them have in my opinion been for the best. I am particularly concerned that some of the changes have come at the expense of teacher development. One of the ways of restoring the balance, I believe, is to re-emphasize the role of the teacher-researcher, emphasize the focus of teacher research on pedagogy and firmly locate this within a whole school context. In this respect it is exciting to see the increasing commitment of the Department for Education and Skills and the Teacher Training Agency to this concept through their initiation and support of the 'Best Practice Research Scholarships' and the 'Teacher Research Grants'. In these final pages I expand a little on this theme and argue, in the spirit of John Fowles, for seeing teacher and school development 'whole'.

Since 1990, in particular, there has been a plethora of comprehensive changes. There have been in many countries seemingly contradictory pressures for centralization (i.e. increasing government control over policy and direction) on the one hand, and de-centralization (i.e. more responsibility for implementation, resource management and evaluation at the school level) on the other. At the same time as national governments have drawn to themselves more power than ever before, the usual infrastructure of support has been eroded and schools are finding themselves increasingly alone in the struggle to take charge of the process of change. All of this has placed enormous pressures on teachers and schools.

Despite this, it is an irony of quite breathtaking proportions that the dramatic increase in educational reform efforts in most Western countries over the past decade is having insufficient impact on levels of student achievement. Admittedly there are pockets of success, such as the claims made for the English National Literacy Strategy by Barber and Sebba (1999). A recent analysis of trends in examination results in English secondary schools, however, suggests only a modest year on year increase even in those schools that are 'improving rapidly' (Gray *et al.* 1999). On the other hand the failure of recent reforms to accelerate student achievement in line with policy objectives has been widely documented (Hopkins and Levin 2000).

A clear indication of the pathology of central policy change was given a few years ago by Milbrey McLaughlin (1990) in her reanalysis of the extensive Rand Change Agent study originally conducted in the United States during the 1970s. McLaughlin (1990: 12) comes to the salutary conclusion that 'policy cannot mandate what matters'. In the paper McLaughlin (1990: 12) puts it this way:

> A general finding of the Change Agent study that has become almost a truism is that it is exceedingly difficult for policy to change practice, especially across levels of government. Contrary to the one-to-one relationship assumed to exist between policy and practice, the Change Agent study demonstrated that the nature, amount, and pace of change at the local level was a product of local factors that were largely beyond the control of higher-level policy makers.

There are in my opinion two key reasons why educational reforms do not in general have the desired impact.

First, many reforms focus on the wrong variables. There is now an increasingly strong research base that suggests that initiatives such as local management of schools, external inspection, organization development, or performance appraisal only indirectly affect student performance. The clear implications for policy are that any strategy to promote student learning needs to give attention to engaging students and parents as active participants, and expanding the teaching and learning repertoires of teachers and students respectively. This is the issue that has been discussed in the previous two chapters.

It is the second reason that provides the focus for the discussion in this chapter. It is that at the time when the community of educational change researchers and practitioners has finally begun to learn something about how ongoing improvement can be fostered and sustained in schools, government policy on education has not taken adequate account of this knowledge about school development. As a consequence, an important source of synergy has been lost and student learning continues to lag behind its potential.

It is instructive to return briefly to McLaughlin's conclusion that 'policy cannot mandate what matters'. In her research she and her colleagues found certain instances where there was a strong correlation between policy and practice. In those situations, however, there was a strong emphasis on implementation strategies that broadly speaking were supportive of the ethos of teacher research and school improvement as described in this book. Those strategies that were generally effective were:

- Concrete, teacher-specific and extended training,
- Classroom assistance from LEA and University,
- Teacher observation in other classrooms, schools or LEAs,
- Regular meetings that focused on practical issues related to teaching and learning,
- Teacher involvement in school improvement planning,
- Local development of classroom materials,
- Head's participation in training.

This finding is much in line with more recent research that suggests that under the right conditions, significant and rapid progress can be made in enhancing the learning of students (Hopkins 2001: Ch 10). In these instances, it is a strong vision coupled to intensive staff development on instructional practices and 'capacity building' that has led to significant increases in levels of student achievement. What is impressive about these examples is that with concerted effort even inner city schools can be turned around. The crucial message appears to be that unless central reforms address the context of teaching and learning, as well as capacity building at the school level, within the context of external support, then the aspirations of reform will never be realised.

The work of Newmann, King and Young (2000) provide another perspective on building learning capacity that complements that of the IQEA project. They argue that professional development is more likely to advance achievement for all students in a school if it addresses not only the learning of individual teachers, but also other dimensions of the organizational capacity of the school. They define *school capacity* as the collective competency of the school as an entity to bring about effective change. They suggest that there are four core components of capacity:

1 *Knowledge, skills and dispositions* of individual staff members;
2 *A Professional learning community* in which staff work collaboratively to set clear goals for student learning, assess how well students are doing,

develop action plans to increase student achievement, whilst being engaged in inquiry and problem-solving;

3 *Program coherence* – 'the extent to which the school's programs for student and staff learning are co-ordinated, focussed on clear learning goals and sustained over a period of time' (p. 5);

4 *Technical resources* – high-quality curriculum, instructional material, assessment instruments, technology, workspace, etc.

Fullan (2000) comments that this four-part definition of school capacity includes 'human capital', that is, the skills of *individuals,* but he concludes that no amount of professional development of individuals will have an impact if certain *organizational* features are not in place. He maintains that one of the key organizational features is 'professional learning communities'. These are the 'social capital' aspects of capacity. In other words, the skills of individuals can only be realized if the *relationships* within the schools are continually developing.

The position being advocated here is similar to the 'new professionalism' proposed by David Hargreaves (1994). His argument was that, paradoxically, much of the recent legislation is having the unintended consequence of eroding the traditional culture of individualism in teaching by forcing structural changes that are generating new forms of collaboration. The 'new professionalism' implies a change in the values and practices of teachers that embraces the ethos of teacher research as structural changes are encouraging a move from 'individualism to collaboration' and from 'hierarchies to teams'. The important point in this context is that once again the skills and aptitudes of the teacher researcher are well suited to this new professional role.

In making his argument, Hargreaves sets out two propositions about the relationship between teacher and school development. The first is that there is little school development without teacher development. The second is that there is little teacher development without school development. The truth of the first proposition is axiomatic. This book and virtually every citation in it are based on that premise. The second proposition is more controversial; but it is at the heart of the difference between this and the original version of the book that was published in 1985. Put simply, I believed then that to improve schools we needed to improve teachers, and to build a community of teacher-researchers. Now I believe that to sustain the ethic of teacher development we need to anchor our work to a whole school context and focus it unrelentingly on the teaching and learning process.

There are two essential strategies or ways or working that need to be implemented if 'professional learning communities' or the 'new professionalism' are to be effectively established. The first are forms of staff development that focus on enhancing classroom practice and the second is the establishing of networks within and outside the school supportive of innovative ways of working. It is to a discussion of each of these that we now turn.

We have not as yet built an infrastructure for staff development within our schools. Such an infrastructure would involve portions of the school week being devoted to staff development activities, such as curriculum development and implementation, new models of teaching, regular observation sessions and on-site coaching. Integral to these activities is a commitment to reviewing one's performance as a prelude to development. It is within this context that classroom research is a fundamental staff development activity.

Bruce Joyce and Beverly Showers' (1995) work on staff development, in particular their peer coaching strategy, has in recent years transformed our thinking on staff development. It is here that there is the closest link with classroom research techniques, especially observation. Joyce and Showers identified a number of key training components which, when used in combination, have much greater power than when used alone. The major components of training are:

- presentation of theory or description of skill or strategy,
- modelling or demonstration of skills or models of teaching,
- practice in simulated and classroom settings,
- structured and open-ended feedback (provision of information about performance), and
- coaching for application (hands-on, in-classroom assistance with the transfer of skills and strategies to the classroom).

Based on this analysis, Joyce and Showers (1984: 85) summarized the 'best knowledge' we have on staff development like this:

- the use of the integrated theory-demonstration-practice feedback training programme to ensure skill development,
- the use of considerable amounts of practice in simulated conditions to ensure fluid control of the new skills,
- the employment of regular on-site coaching to facilitate vertical transfer, and
- the preparation of teachers who can provide one another with the needed coaching.

Joyce (1992) has also distinguished – helpfully in my opinion – between the two key elements of staff development: the workshop and the workplace. The workshop, which is equivalent to the best practice on the traditional INSET course, is where we gain understanding, see demonstrations of the teaching strategy we may wish to acquire, and have the opportunity to practise them in a non-threatening environment. If, however, we wish to transfer these new skills back into the workplace – the classroom and school – then merely attending the workshop is insufficient. The research evidence is very clear that skill acquisition and the ability to transfer vertically to a range of situations requires 'on-the-job support'. This implies changes to the workplace and the way in which we organize staff development in our schools. In particular, this means the opportunity for immediate and sustained practice, collaboration and peer coaching, and studying development and implementation. We cannot achieve these changes in the workplace without, in most cases, drastic alterations to the ways in which we organize our schools. Yet we will not be able to transfer teaching skills from INSET sessions to a range of classrooms without them. Fortunately, at least for teacher researchers, as seen in the examples scattered throughout this book, the workplace conditions they create for themselves mesh with and are similar to the core activities of classroom research.

What is being proposed here is a wide range of staff development activities that represents a fairly sophisticated infrastructure for sustained professional development. A key element in all of this is the provision of in-classroom support or in Joyce and Showers' term 'peer coaching' (Joyce and Showers 1995). It is the facilitation of peer coaching that enables teachers to extend their repertoire of teaching skills and to transfer them from different classroom settings to others.

During the implementation of this approach during our IQEA school improvement projects we have emphasized the use of peer coaching to support student learning (see for example, Joyce *et al.* 1999: Chapter 7). When the refinements noted below are incorporated into a school improvement design, peer coaching can virtually assure 'transfer of training' for everyone:

- Peer coaching teams of two or three are much more effective than larger groups.
- These groups are more effective when the entire staff is engaged in school improvement.
- Peer coaching works better when Heads and Deputies participate in training and practice.
- The effects are greater when formative study of student learning is embedded in the process.

The constellation of staff development activities just described makes the structural link between the collaborative and reflective work of teachers and enhanced levels of student achievement clear and achievable. The staff development focus has the potential to unite both the focus on teaching and learning and capacity building. In highly effective schools it is this that provides the essential infrastructure for school improvement. This may well reflect enhanced 'capacity' within the school, but there is, however, another aspect to building capacity that is reflected in the networks that are established to support innovative work between schools.

There has recently been much international interest in the role of networks in supporting school improvement (e.g. OECD 1999). There are, however, various interpretations of the network concept. Although networks bring together those with like-minded interests, they are more than just opportunities to share 'good practice'. The following definition of networks emerged from an analysis of effective networks identified by the OECD (quotation and discussion in this section based on Hopkins 2000: Chapter 10):

> Networks are purposeful social entities characterised by a commitment to quality, rigour, and a focus on outcomes. They are also an effective means of supporting innovation in times of change. In education, networks promote the dissemination of good practice, enhance the professional development of teachers, support capacity building in schools, mediate between centralised and decentralised structures, and assist in the process of re-structuring and re-culturing educational organisations and systems.

The qualities exhibited by such networks are however not easily acquired. A number of key conditions need to be in place if networks are to realize their potential as agents of educational innovation. In terms of school improvement, a number of conditions for effective networks can be identified:

- *Consistency of values and focus* – it is important that networks have a common aim and purpose, and that the values underpinning the network are well articulated and 'owned' by those involved. This consistency of values and purpose also relates to the need for the focus of the network to be consistent with the overarching policy framework.
- *Clarity of structure* – effective networks are well organized with clear operating procedures and mechanisms for ensuring that maximum participation is achieved within and between schools. These structures promote involvement that is broad-based, preferably with a whole organization or systemic focus, rather than being narrow, limiting or particular.
- *Knowledge creation, utilization and transfer* – the key purpose of networks is to create and disseminate knowledge to support educational improvement and innovation. Such knowledge and practice needs to be based on evidence, focus on the core features of schooling, and are subject to robust quality assurance procedures.
- *Rewards related to learning* – those who belong to networks need to feel that their involvement is worthwhile. Rewards for networking are best related to supporting professional development and the encouraging of learning. Effective networks invest in people.

- *Dispersed leadership and empowerment* – highly effective networks contain skilful people who collaborate and work well together. The skills required by network members are similar to the skill sets associated with effective teams and include a focus on dispersed leadership and empowerment.
- *Adequate resources* – networks need to be adequately resourced particularly in terms of time, finance and human capital. It is not necessarily the quantum of resource that is important, more crucially there needs to be flexibility in the way in which it is deployed.

In line with the argument of this chapter, networks in education have a key role to play in supporting innovation and school improvement. Accordingly, networks need to be regarded as support structures for innovative schools, not only in disseminating 'good practice', but also in overcoming the traditional isolation of schools, and to a certain extent even challenging traditional hierarchical system structures. In the past, most school systems have operated almost exclusively through individual units; be they teachers, departments, schools or local agencies. Such isolation may have been appropriate during times of stability, but during times of change there is a need to 'tighten the loose coupling', to increase collaboration and to establish more fluid and responsive structures. Networks provide an important way of doing this.

To summarize, networks have the potential to support educational innovation and change by:

- Providing a focal point for the dissemination of good practice, the generalizability of innovation and the creation of 'action oriented' knowledge about effective educational practices.
- Keeping the focus on the core purposes of schooling in particular in creating and sustaining a discourse on teaching and learning.
- Enhancing the skill of teachers, leaders and other educators in change agent skills and managing the change process.
- Building capacity for continuous improvement at the local level, and in particular in creating professional learning communities, within and between schools.
- Ensuring that systems of pressure and support are *integrated* not segmented. For example, professional learning communities incorporate pressure and support in a seamless way.
- Acting as a link between the centralized and decentralized schism resulting from many contemporary policy initiatives.

As has been argued at length in this chapter, the main reason why reforms have not had the desired impact is because Government policy on education has not been adequately informed by what is known about teacher and school development. If one issue is certain it is that the future of schooling requires a systemic perspective, which implies a high degree of commitment to school improvement, teacher development and an unrelenting focus on student achievement and learning. Networks, within and outside schools, provide a means for doing just that.

I have tried in these past few pages to demonstrate that classroom research is at the root of key school improvement activities such as acquiring a repertoire of teaching strategies, staff development and networking. I have also argued that because of the recent changes, teachers now, more than ever, need to apply the ethic of teacher research to these areas of professional development. But it increasingly seems to me that teacher research alone is not enough. Reflective classroom practice needs to be linked to whole school development and a focus on teaching and learning.

Schools involved in the Improving the Quality of Education for All project (see Hopkins 2002) for example, use their development plan as an overarching strategy to focus innovative efforts on a limited number of priorities, in a way that generates ownership and galvanizes support. The priorities tend to relate to teaching and classroom organization in a broad sense, and these schools use some form of classroom observation or 'peer coaching' to help staff work together and to learn from each other. The effectiveness of this approach is considerably enhanced when the observation is underpinned by an agreed specification of the teaching strategy to be employed. This provides a 'standard' for the mutual observation, as well as a language for talking about teaching. Indeed, peer coaching is proving to be a powerful means for establishing ownership, of acquiring new teaching strategies and eventually transforming the culture of the school.

Even more power is achieved when schools work together on their school improvement activities. There are now a number of cohorts of schools in this country and elsewhere that are basing their development work on IQEA principles. They are finding that establishing networks, which build in systems for coordination, dissemination and evaluation, provide teachers with greatly increased energy, support, and confidence. We are also finding that a school's improvement work becomes more rapidly institutionalized when it is initiated as part of a network. The Bedfordshire School Improvement Project (BSIP) provides an outstanding example of how such networks support teacher and school development on the one hand, and enhanced learning and achievement of students on the other.

This and the other examples scattered throughout the book suggest that what are needed are powerful and integrative implementation strategies that directly address the nature of teaching and the culture of the school. Our current work with these schools suggests that it is through linking more precise specifications of teaching to classroom research strategies within the context of the development plan that progress is made. Strategies for school improvement that do not link teaching to whole school activities are 'doomed to tinkering'. In short, we need to see teacher and school development whole. When we do this we not only begin to meet the real challenge of educational reform, but we also create classrooms and schools where both our children and their teachers learn.

APPENDIX

Ethics for classroom research

Consider feeding back to students, either those involved in the research or representatives of the student body. Comments following the feedback can provide a further perspective on the findings which can inform subsequent action planning. Action researchers must pay attention to the ethical principles guiding their work. Their actions are deeply embedded in an existing social organization and the failure to work within the general procedures of that organization may not only jeopardize the process of improvement but existing valuable work. Principles of procedure for action research accordingly go beyond the usual concerns for confidentiality and respect for the persons who are the subjects of enquiry and define in addition, appropriate ways of working with other participants in the social organization. The principles outlined below reflect the commitment implicit in the methods of action research to participation and collaborative work, and negotiation within, and ultimately beyond existing social and political circumstances.

Observe protocol: Take care to ensure that the relevant persons, committees and authorities have been consulted, informed and that the necessary permission and approval has been obtained.

Involve participants: Encourage others who have a stake in the improvement you envisage to shape the form of the work.

Negotiate with those affected: Not everyone will want to be directly involved; your work should take account of the responsibilities and wishes of others.

Report progress: Keep the work visible and remain open to suggestions so that unforeseen and unseen ramifications can be taken account of; colleagues must have the opportunity to lodge a protest to you.

Obtain explicit authorization before you observe: For the purposes of recording the activities of professional colleagues or others (the observation of your own students falls outside this imperative provided that your aim is the improvement of teaching and learning).

Obtain explicit authorization before you examine files, correspondence or other documentation: Take copies only if specific authority to do this is obtained.

Negotiate descriptions of people's work: Always allow those described to challenge your accounts on the grounds of fairness, relevance and accuracy.

Negotiate accounts of others' points of view (e.g., in accounts of communication): Always allow those involved in interviews, meetings and written exchanges to require amendments which enhance fairness, relevance and accuracy.

Obtain explicit authorization before using quotations: Verbatim transcripts, attributed observations, excerpts of audio and video recordings, judgements, conclusions or recommendations in reports (written or to meetings).

Negotiate reports for various levels of release: Remember that different audiences demand different kinds of reports; what is appropriate for an informal verbal report to a faculty meeting may not be appropriate for a staff meeting, a report to council, a journal article, a newspaper, a newsletter to parents; be conservative if you cannot control distribution.

Accept responsibility for maintaining confidentiality.

Retain the right to report your work: Provided that those involved are satisfied with the fairness, accuracy and relevance of accounts which pertain to them; and that the accounts do not unnecessarily expose or embarrass those involved; then accounts should not be subject to veto or be sheltered by prohibitions of confidentiality.

Make your principles of procedure binding and known: All of the people involved in your action research project must agree to the principles before the work begins; others must be aware of their rights in the process.

Reprinted, with permission, from Deakin University (Kemmis and McTaggart 1982: 43–4).

References

Abbott, R., Birchenough, M. and Steadman, S. (1988) *GRIDS School Handbooks*, 2nd edn (Primary and Secondary versions). York: Longman for the SCDC.

Acheson, K. and Gall, M. (1992) *Techniques in the Clinical Supervision of Teachers*. New York: Longman.

Adelman, C. (1981) *Uttering, Muttering*. London: Grant McIntyre.

Ainscow, M., Hargreaves, D. H. and Hopkins, D. (1995) Mapping the process of change in schools, *Evaluation and Research in Education*, 9(2): 75–90.

Ainscow, M., Beresford, J., Harris, A. *et al.* (2000) *Creating the Conditions for School Improvement*, 2nd edn. London: David Fulton.

Armstrong, M. (1980) *Closely Observed Children*. London: Writers and Readers.

Armstrong, M. (1982) The story of five stories: An enquiry into children's narrative thought, Unpublished mimeo.

Barber, M. and Sebba, J. (1999) Reflections on progress towards a world class education system, *Cambridge Journal of Education*, 29(2): 183–93.

Barrow, R. (1986) Research into teaching, the conceptual factors, *Educational Research*, 28(3): 220–30.

Becker, H. (1958) Problems of inference and proof in participant observation, *American Sociological Review*, 28: 652–60 (reprinted in McCormick, R. (ed.) (1982) *Calling Education to Account*. London: Heinemann).

Bell, J. (1999) *Doing Your Research Project*. 3rd edn. Buckingham: Open University Press.

Bennett, N. (1976) *Teaching Styles and Pupil Progress*. London: Pergamon Press.

Bennett, N. (1988) The effective primary school teacher; the search for a theory of pedagogy. *Teaching and Teacher Education*, 4(1): 19–30.

Beresford, J. (1998) *Collecting Information for School Improvement*. London: David Fulton.

Beresford, J. (1999) Matching teaching to learning, *Curriculum Journal*, 10(3): 321–44.

Bollen, R. and Hopkins, D. (1987) *School Based Review: Towards a Praxis*. Leuven: ACCO.

Bollington, R. and Bradley, H. (1990) *Training for Appraisal: A Set of Distance Learning Materials*. Cambridge: University of Cambridge Institute of Education.

Bolster, A. (1983) Towards a more effective model of research on teaching, *Harvard Educational Review*, 53(3): 294–308.

Bowen, B., Forsyth, K., Green, J. *et al.* (undated) *Ways of Doing Research in One's Own Classroom*. Cambridge: Cambridge Institute of Education, Ford Teaching Project.

Brophy, J. (1981) Teacher praise: a functional analysis, *Review of Educational Research*, 51: 5–52.

Brophy, J. and Good, T. (1986) Teacher behaviour and student achievement, in M. Wittrock (ed.) *Handbook of Research on Teaching*, 3rd edn. New York: Macmillan.

Cambridge University (1994) *Mapping Change in Schools: The Cambridge Manual of Research Techniques*. Cambridge: UCIE.

Campbell, D. and Stanley, J. (1963) Experimental and quasi-experimental designs for research on teaching, in N. Gage (ed.) *Handbook of Research on Teaching*. Chicago, IL: Rand McNally.

Carr, W. (ed.) (1989) *Quality in Teaching*. Lewes: Falmer Press.

Carr, W. and Kemmis, S. (1986) *Becoming Critical*. Lewes: Falmer Press.

Clift, P., Nuttall, D. and McCormick, R. (1987) *Studies in School Self Evaluation*. Lewes: Falmer Press.

Cogan, M. (1973) *Clinical Supervision*. Boston, MA: Houghton Mifflin.

Congdon, P. (1978) Basic principles of sociometry, *Association of Education Psychologists Journal*, 4(8): 5–9.

Corey, S. (1953) *Action Research to Improve School Practice*. New York: Teacher's College Press.

Creemers, B. (1994) *The Effective Classroom*. London: Cassell.

Croll, P. (1997) *Systematic Classroom Observation*, 2nd edn. Lewes: Falmer Press.

Cronbach, L. J. (1975) Beyond the two disciplines of scientific psychology, *American Psychologist*, 30: 116–27.

Deakin University (1998) *The Action Research Reader*. Victoria: Deakin University Press.

Delamont, S. (1983) *Interaction in the Classroom*. London: Methuen.

Delamont, S. (1984) *Readings on Interaction in the Classroom*. London: Methuen.

Delamont, S. (1992) *Fieldwork in Educational Settings*. Lewes: Falmer Press.

Department of Education and Science (1989) *Planning for School Development*. London: HMSO.

Dillon, J. (1983) Problem solving and findings, *Journal of Creative Behaviour*, 16(2): 97–111.

Downey, L. (1967) *The Secondary Phase of Education*. Boston, MA: Ginn.

Doyle, W. (1987) Research on teaching effects as a resource for improving instruction, in M. Wideen and I. Andrews (eds) *Staff Development for School Improvement*. Lewes: Falmer Press.

Dunn, W. and Swierczek, F. (1977) Planned organizational change: Toward grounded theory, *Journal of Applied Behavioural Science*, 13(2): 135–57.

Ebbutt, D. (1985) Educational action research: Some general concerns and specific quibbles, in R. Burgess (ed.) *Issues in Educational Research*. Lewes: Falmer Press.

Ebbutt, D. and Elliott, J. (eds) (1985) *Issues in Teaching for Understanding*. York: Longman.

Elbaz, F. (1983) *Teacher Thinking – A Study of Practical Knowledge*. London: Croom Helm.

Elliott, J. (1976) *Developing Hypotheses about Classrooms from Teachers' Practical Constructs*. Cambridge: Cambridge Institute of Education, Ford Teaching Project.

Elliott, J. (1991) *Action Research for Educational Change*. Buckingham: Open University Press.

Elliott, J. and Adelman, C. (1976) *Innovation at the Classroom Level: A Case Study of the Ford Teaching Project*. Unit 28, Open University Course E 203: Curriculum Design and Development. Milton Keynes: Open University Educational Enterprises.

Elliott, J. and Ebbutt, D. (1985a) *Facilitating Educational Action Research in Schools*. York: Longman.

Elliott, J. and Ebbutt, D. (eds) (1985b) *Case Studies in Teaching for Understanding*. Cambridge: Cambridge Institute of Education.

Evertson, C. and Harris, A. (1992) What we know about managing classrooms, *Educational Leadership*, April: 74–8.

Fielding, M. (1994) Valuing difference in teachers and learners: Building on Kolb's learning styles to develop a language of teaching and learning, *Curriculum Journal*, 5(3): 393–417.

Fisher, R. (1966) *The Design of Experiments*. 8th edn. Edinburgh: Oliver and Boyd.

Flanders, N. (1970) *Analysing Teaching Behaviour*. Reading, MA: Addison-Wesley.

Fowles, J. (1979) *The Tree*. St Albans: Sumach Press.

Fullan, M. (1993) *Change Forces: Probing the Depths of Educational Reform*. London: Falmer.

Fullan, M. (1997) *What's Worth Fighting For in the Principalship?*, 2nd edn. New York: Teachers College Press.

Fullan, M. (2000) The return of large-scale reform, *Journal of Educational Change*, 2(1): 5–28.

Fullan, M. (2001) *The New Meaning of Educational Change*, 3rd edn. London: Cassell.

Fullan, M. and Hargreaves, A. (1992) *What's Worth Fighting For? Working Together For Your School*. New York: Teachers College Press.

Gage, N. (1978) *The Scientific Basis of the Art of Teaching*. New York: Teachers College Press.

Galton, M. (1978) *British Mirrors*. Leicester: University of Leicester School of Education.

Galton, M., Simon, B. and Croll, P. (1980) *Inside the Primary Classroom*. London: Routledge and Kegan Paul.

Galton, M. (1999) *Inside the Primary Classroom: Twenty Years On*. London: Routledge.

Gardner, H. (1993) *Frames of Mind: The Theory. of Multiple Intelligences*, 2nd edn. London: Fontana Press.

Gibson, R. (1986) *Critical Theory and Education*. London: Hodder and Stoughton.

Glaser, B. and Strauss, A. (1967) *The Discovery of Grounded Theory*. New York: Aldine.

Goldhammer, R., Anderson, R. and Krajewski, R. (1980) *Clinical Supervision: Special Methods for the Supervision of Teachers*, 2nd edn. New York: Holt, Rinehart and Winston.

Good, T. (1989) Using classroom and school research to professionalize teaching. Keynote presentation at International Congress for School Effectiveness and Improvement, Rotterdam, 5th January.

Good, T. and Brophy, J. (1997) *Looking in Classrooms*, 7th edn. Harlow: Longman.

Gray, J., Hopkins, D., Reynolds, D. *et al.* (1999) *Improving Schools. Performance and Potential*. Buckingham: Open University Press.

Halsall, R. (ed.) (1998) *Teacher Research and School Improvement: Opening Doors from the Inside*. Buckingham: Open University Press.

Hamilton, D., Macdonald, B., King, C. *et al.* (eds) (1977) *Beyond the Numbers Game*. Berkeley, CA: McCutchan.

Hammersley, M. (ed.) (1993) *Controversies in Classroom Research*, 2nd edn. Buckingham: Open University Press.

Hammersley, M. and Atkinson, P. (1995) *Ethnography: Principles in Practice*, 2nd edn. London: Routledge.

Hargreaves, A. and Fullan, M. (1998) *What's Worth Fighting For Out There?* Australia: Australian Council for Educational Administration Inc.

Hargreaves, A., Lieberman, A., Fullan, M. and Hopkins, D. (eds) (1998) *International Encyclopaedia of Educational Change*. Dordrecht: Kluwer.

Hargreaves, D. H. (1994) The new professionalism: A synthesis of professional and institutional development, *Teaching and Teacher Education*, 10(4).

Hargreaves, D. H. (1995) School culture, school effectiveness and school improvement, *School Effectiveness and School Improvement*, 6(1): 23–46.

Hargreaves, D. H. and Hopkins, D. (1991) *The Empowered School*. London: Cassell.

Hargreaves, D. H. and Hopkins, D. (eds) (1994) *Development Planning for School Improvement*. London: Cassell.

Hargreaves, D. H., Hopkins, D., Leask, M., Connolly, J. and Robinson, P. (1989) *Planning for School Development*. London: DES.

Hitchcock, G. and Hughes, D. (1995) *Research and the Teacher*, 2nd edn. London: Routledge.

Hook, C. (1981) *Studying Classrooms*. Victoria: Deakin University Press.

Hopkins, D. (1982) Doing research in your own classroom, *Phi Delta Kappan*, 64(4): 274–5.

Hopkins, D. (1984a) Teacher research: Back to the basics, *Classroom Action Research Network Bulletin*, 6: 94–9.

Hopkins, D. (1984b) Towards a methodology for teacher based classroom research, *School Organization*, 4(3): 197–204.

Hopkins, D. (1987) *Improving the Quality of Schooling*. Lewes: Falmer Press.

Hopkins, D. (1988) *Doing School Based Review*. Leuven: ACCO.

Hopkins, D. (1989) *Evaluation for School Development*. Milton Keynes: Open University Press.

Hopkins, D. (2000) Powerful learning, powerful teaching and powerful schools, *The Journal of Educational Change*, 1(2): 135–54.

Hopkins, D. (2001) *School Improvement for Real*. London: Routledge/Falmer.

Hopkins, D. (2002) *Improving the Quality of Education for All*, 2nd edn. London: David Fulton.

Hopkins, D. and Harris, A. (2000) *Creating the Conditions for Teaching and Learning*. London: David Fulton.

Hopkins, D. and Levin, B. (2000) Government policy and school development, *School Leadership and Management*, 20(1): 15–30.

Hopkins, D. and MacGilchrist, B. (1998) Development planning for pupil achievement, *School Leadership and Management*, 18(3): 409–24.

Hopkins, D. and Stern, D. (1996) Quality teachers, quality schools, *Teaching and Teacher Education*, 12(5): 501–17.

Hopkins, D., Ainscow, M. and West, M. (1994) *School Improvement in an Era of Change*. London: Cassell.

Hopkins, D., Bollington, R. and Hewett, D. (1989) Growing up with qualitative research and evaluation, *Evaluation and Research in Education*, 3(2): 61–80.

Hopkins, D., West, M. and Ainscow, M. (1996) *Improving the Quality of Education for All*. London: David Fulton.

Hopkins, D., West, M. and Beresford, J. (1998) Creating the conditions for classroom and teacher development, *Teachers and Teaching*, 4(1): 115–41.

Hopkins, D., West, M., Ainscow, M., Harris, A. and Beresford, J. (1997) *Creating the Conditions for Classroom Improvement*. London: David Fulton.

Hull, C., Rudduck, J. and Sigsworth, A. (1985) *A Room Full of Children Thinking*. York: Longman.

Hustler, D., Cassidy, T. and Cuff, T. (eds) (1986) *Action Research in Classrooms and Schools*. London: Allen & Unwin.

Johnson, D. W. and Johnson, R. T. (1993) *Circles of Learning*. Aedina, MN: Interaction Book Company.

Joyce, B. (1992) Cooperative learning and staff development research: teaching the method with method, *Cooperative Learning*, 12(2): 10–13.

Joyce, B. and Showers, B. (1984) *Transfer of training: The contribution of coaching*. In Hopkins, D. and Wideen, M. (eds) *Alternative Perspectives on School Improvement*. Lewes: Falmer Press.

Joyce, B. and Showers, B. (1995) *Student Achievement Through Staff Development*. White Plains, NY: Longman.

Joyce, B. and Weil, M. (1996) *Models of Teaching*, 5th edn. London: Allyn and Bacon.

Joyce, B. and Calhoun, E. (1997) Learning to teach inductively. Mimeo, Pauma Valley, California.

Joyce, B. and Calhoun, E. (1998) *Learning to Teach Inductively*. Needham Heights, MA: Allyn and Bacon.

Joyce, B., Calhoun, E. and Hopkins, D. (1997) *Models of Learning – Tools for Teaching*. Buckingham: Open University Press.

Joyce, B., Calhoun, E. and Hopkins, D. (1999) *The New Structure of School Improvement: Inquiring Schools and Achieving Students*. Buckingham: Open University Press.

Joyce, B., Calhoun, E. and Hopkins, D. (2002) *Models of Learning – Tools for Teaching*, 2nd edn. Buckingham: Open University Press.

Kemmis, S. (1983) Action research, in T. Husen and T. Postlethwaite (eds) *International Encyclopaedia of Education: Research and Studies*. Oxford: Pergamon.

Kemmis, S. (1988) Action research in retrospect and prospect. In Deakin University *The Action Research Reader*. Victoria: Deakin University Press.

Kemmis, S. and McTaggart, R. (1982) *The Action Research Planner*, 3rd edn. Victoria: Deakin University (1st edn, 1981).

Kolb, D. A. (1984) *Experiential Learning*. Englewood Cliffs, NJ: Prentice-Hall.

Kounin, J. S. (1970) *Discipline and Group Management in Classrooms*. New York: Holt, Rinehart and Winston.

Kyriacou, C. (1997) *Effective Teaching in Schools*, 2nd edn. Cheltenham: Stanley Thornes.

Kyriacou, C. (1998) *Essential Teaching Skills*, 2nd edn. Cheltenham: Stanley Thornes.

Lawton, D. (1989) *Education, Culture and the National Curriculum*. London: Hodder and Stoughton.

Lewin, K. (1946) Action research and minority problems, *Journal of Social Issues*, 2: 34–46.

Lincoln, Y. and Guba, E. (1985) *Naturalistic Inquiry*. Beverly Hills, CA: Sage.

Lortie, D. (1975) *School Teacher*. Chicago, IL: University of Chicago Press.

Louis, K. S. and Miles, M. (1992) *Improving the Urban High School*. London: Cassell.

Macbeath, J. (1999) *Schools Must Speak for Themselves*. London: Routledge.

MacDonald, B. and Walker, R. (eds) (1974) *Innovation, Evaluation Research and the Problem of Control*. Norwich: CARE, University of East Anglia Press.

MacGilchrist, B., Mortimore, P., Savage, J. and Beresford, C. (1995) *Planning Matters*. London: Paul Chapman.

MacGilchrist, B., Myers, K. and Reed, J. (1997) *The Intelligent School*. London: Paul Chapman.

Magee, B. (1973) *Popper*. London: Fontana/Collins.

May, N. and Rudduck, J. (1983) *Sex Stereotyping and the Early Years of Schooling.* Norwich: University of East Anglia Press.

McCormick, R. and James, M. (1989) *Curriculum Evaluation in Schools,* 2nd edn. London: Routledge.

McKernan, J. (1996) *Curriculum Action Research,* 2nd edn. London: Kogan Page.

McLaughlin, M. W. (1990) The Rand Change Agent study revisited: macro perspectives, micro realities, *Educational Researcher,* 19(9): 11–16.

McMahon, A., Bolam, R., Abbott, R. and Holly, P. (1984) *GRIDS School Handbooks* (Primary and Secondary versions). York: Longman for the Schools Council.

McNiff, J. (1992) *Action Research: Principles and Practice.* London: Routledge.

Miles, M. and Huberman, M. (1984) Drawing valid meaning from qualitative data: Toward a shared craft, *Educational Researcher,* 13(5): 20–30.

Miles, M. and Huberman, M. (1994) *Qualitative Data Analysis: A Sourcebook of New Methods.* Beverly Hills, CA: Sage.

Miujs, D. and Reynolds, D. (2001) *Effective Teaching. Research and Practice.* London: Paul Chapman.

Mortimore, P. (1993) School Effectiveness and the Management of Effective Learning and Teaching. *School Effectiveness and School Improvement,* 4(4): 290–310.

Newmann, F., King, B. and Young, S. P. (2000) Professional development that addresses school capacity: Lessons from urban elementary schools. Paper presented to Annual Meeting of the American Educational Research Association, 3rd April, New Orleans.

Nixon, J. (ed.) (1981) *A Teacher's Guide to Action Research.* London: Grant and McIntyre.

OECD (1999) *Innovating Schools.* Paris: OECD/CERI.

Office For Standards in Education (1998) *School Evaluation Matters,* London: OFSTED.

Oja, S. N. and Smulyan, L. (1989) *Collaborative Action Research.* Lewes: Falmer Press.

Open University (1976) *Personality and Learning, Course E201.* Milton Keynes: Open University.

Patterson, J., Purkey, S. C. and Parker, J. (1986) *Productive School Systems for a Non-rational World.* Alexandria, VA: ASCD.

Patton, M. Q. (1990) *Qualitative Evaluation Methods.* Beverly Hills, CA: Sage.

Polanyi, M. (1973) *Personal Knowledge.* Reprinted. London: Routledge and Kegan Paul.

Pring, R. (1978) Teacher as researcher, in D. Lawton, P. Gordon, M. Ing *et al.* (eds) *Theory and Practice of Curriculum Studies.* London: Routledge and Kegan Paul.

Rapoport, R. (1970) Three dilemmas in action research, *Human Relations,* 23: 1–11.

Robson, C. (1993) *Real World Research.* Oxford: Blackwells.

Rowland, S. (1984) *The Enquiring Classroom: An Introduction to Children's Learning.* Lewes: Falmer Press.

Rudduck, J. (1981) *Making the Most of the Short Inservice Course.* London: Methuen.

Rudduck, J. (ed.) (1982) *Teachers in Partnership: Four Studies of Inservice Collaboration.* York: Longman.

Rudduck, J. (1984) Introducing innovation to pupils, in D. Hopkins and M. Wideen (eds) *Alternative Perspectives on School Improvement.* Lewes: Falmer Press.

Rudduck, J. (1991) *Innovation and Change.* Buckingham: Open University Press.

Rudduck, J. and Hopkins, D. (eds) (1985) *Research as a Basis for Teaching.* London: Heinemann.

Rudduck, J. and Sigsworth, A. (1985) Partnership supervision, in D. Hopkins and K. Reid (eds) *Rethinking Teacher Education.* London: Croom Helm.

Sandford, N. (1970) Whatever happened to action research? *Journal of Social Issues,* 26(4): 3–23.

Schön, D. (1991) *The Reflective Practitioner*. New York: Basic Books.

Schwandt, T. and Halpern, E. (1988) *Linking Auditing and MetaEvaluation*. Beverly Hills, CA: Sage.

Sharan, S. and Shachar, H. (1988) *Language and Learning in the Co-operative Classroom*. New York: Springer-Verlag.

Simon, A. and Boyer, E. (1975) *Mirrors for Behaviour: An Anthology of Classroom Observation Instruments*. Philadelphia, PA: Research for Better Schools Inc.

Simons, H. (1982) Suggestions for a school self evaluation based on democratic principles, in R. McCormick (ed.) *Calling Education to Account*. London: Heinemann.

Simons, H. (1987) *Getting to Know Schools in a Democracy*. Lewes: Falmer Press.

Smith, L. and Geoffrey, W. (1968) *The Complexities of an Urban Classroom*. New York: Holt, Rinehart and Wilson.

Stake, R. E. (1995) *The Art of Case Study Research*. Thousand Oaks, CA: Sage.

Stenhouse, L. (1970) *The Humanities Project*. London: Heinemann. (Revised edition by Rudduck, J. (1983) Norwich: University of East Anglia Press.)

Stenhouse, L. (1975) *An Introduction to Curriculum Research and Development*. London: Heinemann.

Stenhouse, L. (1979) Using research means doing research, in H. Dahl, A. Lysne and P. Rand (eds) *Spotlight on Educational Research*. Oslo: University Press.

Stenhouse, L. (1980) Product or process: A response to Brian Crittenden, *New Education*, 2(1): 137–40.

Stenhouse, L. (1983) *Authority, Education and Emancipation*. London: Heinemann.

Stenhouse, L. (1984) Artistry and teaching: The teacher as focus of research and development, in D. Hopkins and M. Wideen (eds) *Alternative Perspectives on School Improvement*. Lewes: Falmer Press.

Stoll, L. and Fink, D. (1996) *Changing our Schools*. Buckingham: Open University Press.

Strauss, A. (1987) *Qualitative Analysis for Social Scientists*. Cambridge: Cambridge University Press.

Strauss, A. and Corbin, J. (1998) *Basics of Qualitative Research*, 2nd edn. London: Sage.

Walker, R. (1989) *Doing Research*. London: Routlege.

Walker, R. and Adelman, C. (1990) *A Guide to Classroom Observation*. London: Routledge.

Webb, R. (ed.) (1990) *Practitioner Research in the Primary School*. Lewes: Falmer Press.

Whitman, W. (1855/1959) *Leaves of Grass*. New York: Viking.

Winter, R. (1989) *Learning from Experience*. Lewes: Falmer Press.

Wood, D. (1998) *How Children Think and Learn*. Oxford: Basil Blackwell.

Index